LIVING
IN A **WORLD** WITH NO
CONSCIENCE

LIVING
IN A **WORLD** WITH NO
CONSCIENCE

Has America Reached the Point of No Return?

M IKE W INGFIELD

WESTBOW
PRESS®
A DIVISION OF THOMAS NELSON
& ZONDERVAN

WestBow Press books may be ordered through booksellers or by contacting:

WestBow Press
A Division of Thomas Nelson & Zondervan
1663 Liberty Drive
Bloomington, IN 47403
www.westbowpress.com
1 (866) 928-1240

Because of the dynamic nature of the Internet, any web addresses or links contained in this book may have changed since publication and may no longer be valid. The views expressed in this work are solely those of the author and do not necessarily reflect the views of the publisher, and the publisher hereby disclaims any responsibility for them.

Any people depicted in stock imagery provided by Getty Images are models, and such images are being used for illustrative purposes only. Certain stock imagery © Getty Images.

Scripture taken from the King James Version of the Bible.

This book is a work of non-fiction. Unless otherwise noted, the author and the publisher make no explicit guarantees as to the accuracy of the information contained in this book and in some cases, names of people and places have been altered to protect their privacy.

ISBN: 978-1-9736-5287-8 (sc)
ISBN: 978-1-9736-5289-2 (hc)
ISBN: 978-1-9736-5288-5 (e)

Library of Congress Control Number: 2019901359

Print information available on the last page.

WestBow Press rev. date: 2/6/2019

ACKNOWLEDGMENTS

First, I must thank my Lord for saving me and calling me into the ministry. I am deeply grateful to my dear wife, Joyce, who has faithfully stood beside me and supported me in this ministry for more than 50 years. I could have accomplished nothing without her prayers, encouragement, and help. I am also deeply grateful to my professors at Grace Seminary who impacted my life more than forth years ago with their faithful biblical instruction and godly examples.

I would like to thank all of those who over the past few years have encouraged me to write on this subject. I have been blessed to witness the overwhelming influence that the preaching on the conscience has had on those who have opened their hearts to the profound and powerful impact of the Word of God.

I also wish to give thanks to four people who labored with me in preparing this book. Darrell Gleason, thank you for your expert advice as an editor of a local newspaper. I deeply appreciate your dedication to provide your faithful service and many hours in pouring over this manuscript. You are a very dear friend and valuable board member of our board of directors.

I want to thank Naomi Chaney for the many hours she gave while editing the manuscript of this book. Thank you for your patience and dedication to carefully examine the grammar and form, making this a better publication for the glory of our Lord. I am so thankful for you and your husband Dennis, for the many years of friendship and fellowship we have enjoyed. I especially enjoyed our trip together in Israel several years ago.

I am also deeply grateful to Pastor Larry Williams, a very dear friend and colleague in the ministry. Thank you so much for your encouraging and helpful insights, and editing suggestions with the grammar and form for this book. Thank you for your sacrificial service to me and our Lord with the publication of this book. I am deeply grateful to you for your service.

I wish to thank Donovan Haynes for creating the cover for this book. Thank you very much for your counsel and insight. Your skills and practical wisdom continue to amaze me. You are not only my son-in-law, but a dear friend and valuable board member of our board of directors. Your assistance in this ministry has been a real encouragement to me.

Lastly, I thank the entire staff at Westbow Press for their help in the publication of this book.

DEDICATION

This book is dedicated to my father, the late Rev. James H. Wingfield, Jr. (1925–2008) Dad was more than a just my earthly father, he was my godly spiritual mentor.

Dad was born on September 26, 1925 to the late James H., Sr. and Lucy Wingfield. He grew up in poverty during the Great Depression with his parents, one sister and three brothers. His parents were tenant farmers in Bedford and Roanoke County, Virginia. Dad's father passed away in a tragic farming accident when he was only fourteen years old. Consequently, he abandoned his academic studies at school and assumed the role of the major care-taker for his widowed mother and siblings still living on the tenant farm. At age eighteen he was drafted into the U.S. Army and served his country during World War II. After he returned home, Dad married my mother, Mildred C. King, in 1947. Two years later, I was born.

In the spring of 1958, my parents made an important decision to build their own house. After the sale of my childhood home, we rented a property only one block from a church located about one mile from our future home site. In a matter of days, the pastor of the church visited our home and invited my family to church. Upon hearing the gospel, my parents, sister, and I received Christ. Our lives as individuals and a family were never the same.

My Dad's life drastically changed. Before he received Christ, he was a good husband and father. He did not have any bad habits. He did not have a wicked mouth. But, when he got saved, he fell in love with Jesus and the Bible. Dad spent time alone with God in his Bible every morning before he went to work. For many years in my parents' home after Dad's conversion, I recall coming to the breakfast table every morning and finding Dad's empty coffee cup and his soiled and worn Bible still open to the last passage he was reading before he went out the door. I knew he had spent time with the Lord early that morning before going to work. Obviously, this had a profound impact upon me.

Dad rapidly grew in his faith. He acquired his GED and began attending a local Bible institute. In just a few years he began to teach the adult Sunday School class in the church where we were saved. A few years after this, he began to preach in homes and rescue missions. During this time he became an effective soul winner, leading many people to saving faith in Jesus Christ. Finally, he decided to plant a church in a nearby community, which grew rapidly in its early years.

Witnessing these changes and the spiritual growth of my Dad changed my life. I began, at the age of nine to read and study the Bible. I started teaching Sunday school when I was fourteen. I started preaching when I was eighteen and pastoring when I was twenty-one. Humanly speaking, God changed my life through the godly influence of my Dad.

I am deeply indebted to my Dad for helping me develop a healthy conscience and instill the fear of God in my life at an early age. I can honestly say that in my teen years, it was not only the fear of God that kept me from evil, but also a healthy, loving fear of my Dad.

In light of this, I think it is only fitting that I dedicate this book to his loving and enduring memory. I look forward to seeing him again when we are both in the presence of the Lord.

CONTENTS

Introduction xi

CHAPTER 1   The Collapse of the American Culture 1

CHAPTER 2   What is the Conscience? 7

CHAPTER 3   What Influences the Conscience? 19

CHAPTER 4   What Makes the Conscience Weak? 31

CHAPTER 5   What Makes the Conscience Strong? 35

CHAPTER 6   Living in a Nation of Fools 43

CHAPTER 7   Living in a Culture of Deception 57

CHAPTER 8   Violence and the End of a Culture 67

CHAPTER 9   Pornography – The Conscience Killer 79

CHAPTER 10   Striving for Moral Purity in a Sex-Crazy World 93

CHAPTER 11   Living in a Demonic Society 107

CHAPTER 12   America and the Spiritual Point of No Return 125

CHAPTER 13   My Prayer: May God Have Mercy on America 137

Endnotes 147

About the Author 149

Other Publications and Ministry
Opportunities by the Author 151

INTRODUCTION

The book you hold in your hand represents forty-six years of prayers, tears, observations, and most importantly, the study of Scripture to find biblical answers concerning the societal collapse of America. I love people and I love America. I am torn when I look over my nation and see the plight of its families, communities, and churches. In the last twenty-one years of my life I have traveled across America to speak in hundreds of churches about the signs of the imminent return of Jesus Christ to take His church home to heaven. In the course of this calling and privilege, I have developed a heavy heart for America.

I believe we live at a tragic time when most Americans, even those who claim to be conservative evangelical Christians, are overwhelmed with the frantic pace of their lifestyles. Consequently, they have failed to prayerfully pause long enough to look at the spiritual condition of our nation through the lens of Scripture. Obviously, those who do not know Jesus Christ are oblivious to where we are and what is about to transpire in America and our world. However, I am also convinced an overwhelming number of believers, including pastors, do not grasp the gravity of what is taking place in America and the global culture. It is my prayer that this book might provide us with a much needed wake-up call!

Jesus warned us that the last days would be "as the days of Noah" (Matthew 24:37). Within the context of this statement, our Lord was saying that in the final hour of this age, people would be so pre-occupied with their daily routine they would be oblivious to the impending judgment of God that would fall upon them. Think about it. Only twenty-four hours before the flood in Noah's day, people must have had some visible warnings that judgment was about to occur. After all, Noah had preached about this judgment for 120 years. However, people blindly missed the warnings and it cost them their lives.

A study of Genesis 6 reveals the global population in Noah's world had reached a spiritual point of no return that demanded the imminent judgment of God. In this book, I will attempt to demonstrate that America and our world are extremely close to reaching this same spiritual point of no return. At the heart of this is the silencing of the collective conscience of our nation and world. God has warned, "My spirit will not always strive with man" (Genesis 6:3). What does this mean? What do we need to do? I hope to help you discover the vital answers to these questions.

After a brief introduction in chapter one, the following four chapters explore what the Bible has to say about the human conscience. In these chapters, I will endeavor to give a biblical understanding to the problem and solution that we are facing as we watch the cultural collapse of our country. In chapters six thru eleven, I will identify and examine six spiritual dangers that always accompany the silencing of the collective conscience in a culture. These six spiritual dangers are: foolishness, deception, violence, pornography, immorality, and demonic influence. In these chapters, I also will offer a biblical prescription for dealing with these deadly dangers. In chapter twelve we will explore the Bible to answer the critical question: "Has America reached the spiritual point of no return?" Finally, in the last chapter I share a prayer for America that God has laid on my heart and in my soul. I hope that this prayer will stir you to get on your knees and pray for our nation. We must seek the face of God for our people, families, communities, churches, and nation. I believe it is America's only hope!

I pray that as you read this book, the Lord will open your understanding to the urgent spiritual needs of our nation and world. I pray that the Lord will enable you to learn how you can strengthen your conscience and the consciences of those around you. May God give us wisdom as we examine our lives in light of the Word given to us by the One who created us and will soon judge us.

CHAPTER 1

The Collapse of the American Culture

"But evil men and seducers shall wax worse and
worse, deceiving and being deceived."
2 Timothy 3:13

I AM ALARMED AND SHOCKED AT THE SUSTAINED RAPID collapse of the American culture. America is in a present state of spiritual, moral, social, economic, and political upheaval. It is as if our world has gone mad! The American culture is like a runaway train careening down a steep mountain with no one in the engineer's seat. It is like a plane that has just lost its instrument panel, leaving the pilot to fly in the fog over rugged mountain terrain.

Marriage and the home are collapsing around us. Children, teens, and young adults are in a state of defiance, rebelling against all authority in the home, community, church, and nation. There is a growing racial tension and hatred, leading to assaults upon our police. It is apparent that a spirit of lawlessness is sweeping across our nation.

Each day there seems to be another senseless act of violence whereby innocent people are brutally murdered. These attacks are taking place in homes, schools, commercial centers, airports, synagogues, and churches. It is apparent that respect for human life is rapidly disintegrating. As we shall see in this book, this is a frightening sign of the self-destruction of a nation.

The moral collapse of America is terrifying. Militant homosexuals, parading transgenders, and aggressive pedophiles are multiplying at an alarming rate. An overwhelming number of Americans are daily filling their minds with pornographic gratification. Millions are clamoring for sexual freedom, when in reality they are enslaving themselves to a lifestyle that is destroying them physically, spiritually, economically, mentally, and morally.

More Americans than ever before are taking medications to deal with their mental anxieties, worries, traumas, and disorders. The complications of our society are bringing people, young and old, to the brink of mental collapse. Millions have developed drug and alcohol addictions in an attempt to numb their pain. And, as a last resort, some have elected to end it all and commit suicide.

Our country is filled with a spirit of hatred, violence, lawlessness, and deception. At the same time, foolishness and arrogance seem to permeate a greater majority of the American public. There is a growing sense of suspicion and disrespect toward each other that is ripping the nation apart. We are politically, morally, spiritually, and racially divided. While this present state of crucial deterioration has been going on for several decades, it is gaining momentum, moving America toward national suicide.

The very fabric of moral integrity and decency that were the foundation of this nation during my childhood years has disintegrated. There appears to be a wholesale abandonment of the values that sustained America for more than two hundred years. There seems to be a growing rejection of reverence for God, the Bible, marriage, biblical morality, and the rule of law. Long ago, the psalmist said, "If the foundations be destroyed, what can the righteous do?" (Psalm 11:3) In the context of this psalm, he speaks of a time when the wicked will have the upper hand and will attack the righteous. In other words, the culture will reach a tipping point when right becomes wrong and wrong becomes right. God has warned, "Woe unto them that call evil good, and good evil; that put darkness for light, and light for darkness; that put bitter for sweet, and sweet for bitter" (Isaiah 5:20)! When this happens, it will lead to the suicide of that culture. When people no longer recognize sin and have no sense of wrong, their sin will enslave them, blind them, deceive them, and destroy them. This spiritual insanity will cause them to rush with great passion toward the door marked "death."

At the heart of all of this is the elevation of humanism, which promotes self, and the willful rejection of God and His laws. At best, the people in this culture may pay lip service to the reality of God, but practically they have made themselves god. What they think and how they feel drive them to choose their lifestyles and pursue their self-appointed goals. "The wicked, through the pride of his countenance, will not seek after God: God is not in all his thoughts" (Psalm 10:4).

Does the Bible hold the answer to how this has happened in America? And if it does, what can we do to warn others and protect ourselves from falling into this same deadly trap that has ensnared so many around us?

That is the purpose of this book. I am sixty-nine years old and have been in the ministry for forty-six years. I must confess that what I am about to share with you is rarely understood in Christian circles today or taught in churches. I am absolutely convinced that if believers could grasp what Scripture teaches about their God-given conscience and how it works, they would know how to pray and to have victory over the evil that is all around them – and even in them.

The plight of our nation is being exacerbated by the church, which is out of touch with the urgency needed to address the collapse of our culture. Many pastors and church leaders are locked in their own traditional ministry treadmills, unaware of the real condition of the world all around them. The Lord has not called us to develop a monastic type of ministry that is isolated from the world. He wants us to be keenly aware of the spiritual needs of the people around us. Jesus modeled this in His discipleship training of His twelve disciples. He was constantly attempting to train them to see the needs of the people around them. For example, after He spoke with the Samaritan woman at the well in John 4, His disciples asked Him why He talked with her. He said to them:

"Lift up your eyes, and look on the fields; for they are white already to harvest" (John 4:35). He wanted them to see the spiritual needs of this people group that the Jewish people despised and rejected. During His earthly ministry Jesus constantly reached out to the outcasts of His day. And because of this, the religious bigots of His day rebuked Him.

It is vital for all believers to have a biblical worldview. A biblical worldview means we are constantly looking through the lens of Scripture to see our world as it really is. This also takes into account the times in which we live in light of God's eternal plans as detailed in prophetic Scripture. When the apostle Paul wrote to the church at Thessalonica about the conditions that would be prevalent at the time of the Rapture, He commended them for their awareness of the nature of that day. They had a proper worldview about the times surrounding the end of the age. He said, "But ye, brethren, are not in [spiritual] darkness, that that day should overtake you as a thief. Ye are all the children of the light [the prophetic revelation], and the children of the day: we are not of the night, nor of darkness" (1 Thessalonians 5:4-5).

While speaking about the end times, Daniel, almost six hundred years earlier, wrote, "Many shall be purified, and made white, and tried; but the wicked shall do wickedly: and none of the wicked shall understand, but the wise shall understand" (Daniel 12:10). The Bible is indicating that those who have an understanding of prophetic Scripture will be wise and understand the times in which they live.

The message of the end times and the details of the second coming of Christ have been absent from many of the pulpits of America for several decades. Many church leaders have concluded that prophetic Scripture is not practical or irrelevant to our times. What these church leaders do not understand is that eschatology is the glue that binds all the biblical doctrines together. If we are not focused on the personal and practical end of our faith, then we have no hope. While writing about the resurrection of Christ and its connection to the hope of our resurrection, the apostle Paul wrote, "If in this life only we have hope in Christ, we are of all men most miserable" (1 Corinthians 15:19).

It is my prayer that this book will enable you to develop a true biblical view of the American culture. I believe that when we examine the prophetic Scripture and what the Bible teaches about what happens to individuals and cultures with a seared conscience, it will give us a sense of urgency. America and our world are ripe for the judgment of God, just as they were in the days of Noah and Sodom and Gomorrah.

As I write this, an 1869 gospel song by Fanny Crosby comes to my mind. It seems to be so fitting for us to consider as we think about the ministry set before us at this time.

Rescue the perishing, care for the dying,
Snatch them in pity from sin and the grave;
Weep o'er the erring one, lift up the fallen,
Tell them of Jesus, the mighty to save.

Refrain:
Rescue the perishing, care for the dying,
Jesus is merciful, Jesus will save.

Though they are slighting Him, still He is waiting,
Waiting the penitent child to receive;
Plead with them earnestly, plead with them gently;
He will forgive if they only believe.

Down in the human heart, crushed by the tempter,
Feelings lie buried that grace can restore;
Touched by a loving heart, wakened by kindness,
Cords that were broken will vibrate once more.

Rescue the perishing, duty demands it;
Strength for thy labor the Lord will provide;
Back to the narrow way patiently win them;
Tell the poor wand'rer a Savior has died.

CHAPTER 2

What is the Conscience?

"For when the Gentiles, which have not the law, do by nature
the things contained in the law, these having not the law,
are a law unto themselves; Which show the work of the law
written in their hearts, their conscience also bearing witness,
and their thoughts the mean while accusing
or else accusing one another."
Romans 2:14-15

THE UNDERSTANDING OF THE CONSCIENCE AND HOW it functions is extremely difficult to grasp. The conscience is hard for our finite minds to comprehend because it is not a physical reality we can tangibly see or touch. According to the Bible, the conscience is a part of the spirit, the heart, and the soul of man. This is what the Bible refers to as the invisible inner man. In the Old Testament, many times the Hebrew word "leb" is usually translated "heart." However, it is also frequently used as a reference to the conscience. As John MacArthur observes, "Thus when Moses recorded that Pharaoh 'hardened his heart' (Exod. 8:15), he was saying that Pharaoh had steeled his conscience against God's will. When Scripture speaks of a tender heart (cf. 2 Chr. 34:27), it refers to a sensitive conscience. The 'upright in heart' (Ps. 7:10) are those with pure consciences." [1]

In order to understand this aspect of man, we must turn to the Bible for insight. Human psychology sheds little light. Psychology comes from two Greek words that mean "soul word." In other words, modern psychology is man's feeble attempt to understand the soul or inner man in light of his own experiences and reasoning. It is an attempt by man to understand who we are, without giving any recognition to God or His divine revelation. The Bible clearly teaches that man does not have the ability to do this without God's revelation. "There is a way which seemth right unto a man, but the end thereof are the ways of death" (Proverbs 14:12). The Bible also declares, "The ways of a man are clean in his own eyes, but the LORD weigheth the spirits" (Proverbs 16:2). Man, in and of himself, is totally blind to his real nature. He lives in self-deception, lying to himself about himself all the time. Listen to what the Holy Spirit caused the prophet Jeremiah to write, "The heart is deceitful above all things, and desperately wicked, who can know it? I the LORD search the heart, I try his reins [mind], even to give every man according to his ways, and according to the fruit of his doings" (Jeremiah 17:9-10). Quite frankly, this revelation about who we really are is difficult for us to accept. It really is an attack upon our pride. We like to think that we are basically good. However, the Bible teaches that without God's help, we are hopelessly trapped and enslaved to our twisted, deceptive, and complex sin nature.

Our understanding of the conscience and how it functions is extremely important. It is at the core of living the victorious Christian life. The apostle Paul identified the possession of a "good conscience" as an essential element in the believer's aim or goal of serving God with a pure heart and sincere faith (1 Timothy 1:5, 19). While giving his testimony and defending his faith before the Roman governor Felix, at Caesarea, Paul commented, "And herein do I exercise myself, to always have a conscience void of offence toward God and toward men" (Acts 24:16). This means that when we strive for a good conscience, we are allowing the Holy Spirit to guide us so we do not sin against God or man. This is the heart of the law of God. In the Ten Commandments, the first four point to man's relationship with

God and the last six deal with man's relationship with man. When Jesus answered the question about the greatest commandment in the law, He said, "Thou shalt love the Lord thy God with all thy heart, and with all thy soul, and with all thy mind. This is the first and great commandment. And the second is like unto it. Thou shalt love thy neighbor as thyself. On these two commandments hang all the law and the prophets" (Matthew 22:37-39). The Bible teaches that our love for man is a demonstration or proof of our love for God. "If a man say, I love God, and hateth his brother, he is a liar; for he that loveth not his brother whom he hath seen, how can he love God whom he hath not seen? And this commandment have we from him, that he who loveth God love his brother also" (1 John 4:20-21).

You and I are "fearfully and wonderfully made" (Psalm 139:14). We were created by God in the womb in the image of God (Genesis 1:26-27). Only human beings have been created in the image of God. Unlike other creatures, man was made as an eternal, intelligent person with emotions, a will, a soul/spirit, and a conscience. In essence, man is not just a physical person, but mysteriously possesses the gift of being a spirit being. Part of what makes man unique is he, like God, is a moral person. God is good, pure, just, and righteous. God is not evil. He does not sin. God is infinitely good in the purest sense of divine holiness. Therefore, when God created Adam and Eve, He made them like God – in His image. Before the fall, they were innocent and pure in their deeds and motives. However, God also chose to make Adam and Eve, like Himself, to possess a personal will. So, God created them with a perfect conscience and a personal will. As long as they worshipped and obeyed God, their conscience gave joyful approval of their actions, thoughts, and motives. For example, the Bible states, "And they were both naked, the man and his wife, and were not ashamed" (Genesis 2:25).

As innocent, untested persons, God gave Adam and Eve clear and simple instructions to maintain their daily walk with Him in the Garden of Eden. They were to multiply and populate the earth (Genesis 1:28). Like God, they were to exercise God's authority to maintain His creation for His glory (Genesis 1:26, 28:2:15). And, they were commanded to eat freely of all the fruit trees in the garden, except "the tree of knowledge of good and evil" (Genesis 2:16, 17).

God told Adam what would happen if they ate the forbidden fruit, "for in the day that thou eatest thereof thou shalt surely die" (Genesis 2:17). When Adam and Eve ate the prohibited fruit, they did not suddenly physically die, but they immediately spiritually died. In the Bible, the word death means separation. When Adam and Eve ate the forbidden fruit, their unique relationship with God was broken. Instead of being sons of God with a daily precious relationship and fellowship with Him, they instantly became "aliens" and "enemies" of God (Romans 5:10; Colossians 1:21). Although they remained creatures in the image of God, that image was marred by their disobedience. They could no longer make decisions based upon reasoning that was founded in their personal understanding and complete trust in their holy God. Their God-given intellect and conscience were now flawed. Their thought process was focused on self rather than on God and His revelation. This radical and sudden spiritual change in man is known as "the fall." Mankind lost their ability to glorify or please God. They now had fallen from their Creator's purpose – to please Him in all they do.

This was instantly revealed by how they looked at each other. After they ate the fruit, the Bible says, "And the eyes of them both were opened, and they knew that they were naked: and they sewed fig leaves together, and made themselves aprons" (Genesis 3:7). Notice that before they sinned, the Bible states, "And they were naked, the man and his wife, and they were not ashamed" (Genesis 2:25). What made the difference? Before their disobedience, they were spiritually alive and trusting in God, who had told them to "be fruitful and multiply" (Genesis 1:28). However, after their act of disobedience, they were spiritually dead toward God and only thought in terms of gratifying self rather than God. Therefore, they looked at one another differently. Before the fall they looked at each other in terms of pleasing God in their sexual activities. In essence, their conscience gave approval of God's blessings on their acts and thoughts. However, after the fall they began to look at one another in terms of lust with a desire to please self. Consequently, their God-given conscience caused them to be ashamed of their actions and thoughts.

Since the fall of man, all human beings have entered the world in the same spiritual condition as Adam and Eve. All babies come into this world with a marred image of God. They are conceived in sin (Psalm 51:5). They are born alienated from God and do not have the capacity to spiritually please Him. The spiritual DNA that is transferred to them at the moment of conception determines they will be born with a twisted intellect and conscience that has been impacted by the sins of their forefathers. While giving Israel the Ten Commandments, the LORD informed them that He visits "the iniquity of the fathers upon the children unto the third and fourth generation of them that hate me; And showing mercy unto thousands of them that love me, and keep my commandments" (Exodus 20:5-6). Therefore, as we consider the conscience of man, we must be continually reminded that Adam and Eve had a pure conscience before the fall occurred. As a result of the fall, no one has possessed a pure and undefiled conscience since.

Everyone is born with a conscience. This is one of the evidences that mankind is created in the image of God. This is not true of other creatures. Only man has a conscience. Only human beings are moral beings. Animals do not have a conscience and are not moral beings.

What is the conscience and how does it function? Again, understanding the spiritual part of man, which includes the conscience, is difficult for us to grasp. As previously mentioned, we must totally rely upon Scripture to enable us to understand what the conscience is and how it was intended to function. "But the natural man receiveth not the things of the Spirit of God: for they are foolishness unto him: neither can he know them, because they are spiritually discerned" (1 Corinthians 2:14). When God created Adam and Eve, He created them with spiritual life and the capacity to know and enjoy God and His spiritual laws. He wrote these laws upon their conscience. These laws were good, perfect, and righteous because God is good, perfect, and righteous. God does not just simply declare something to be "good." God's goodness reflects His perfect character and will. The Bible repeatedly tells us God is the

God of truth [reality]. This is what Jesus declared, when He said, "I am the way, the truth, and the life" (John 14:6).

Each human being is born as a sinner. They have a flawed conscience that gives them some limited sense of right and wrong. At the same time, each child is born with a sin nature [a personal will that is bent on rebellion against God and their God-given conscience]. In Romans 1, the apostle Paul wrote to the church in Rome to remind them they were living in a pagan culture in total rebellion against God and His laws. He said, "For the wrath of God is revealed from heaven against all ungodliness and unrighteousness of men, who hold [suppress] the truth [in their conscience] in unrighteousness. Because that which may be known of God is manifest in them [their conscience]; for God hath showed it unto them" (Romans 1:18, 19).

The Bible teaches that the believer lives in constant internal war because his conscience is calling him to obey God's law. On the other hand, his personal and sinful will is warring against the conscience by calling upon the believer to gratify self rather than God! This is the basis for understanding the struggle against sin in the believer's life as described by the apostle Paul in Romans 7:7-25. The greatest enemy the believer faces is not Satan, his demons, or the world. Our greatest enemy is the inner sin-nature which is at "war against the soul" (1 Peter 2:11). Clearly, I am my own worst enemy, according to the Bible!

Isn't it ironic that when Satan tempted Eve, he lied to her by leaving the impression that if she ate the prohibited fruit she would be like God and have a grasp of good and evil? (Genesis 3:5) Before she disobeyed God, she was walking in fellowship with the God of truth. Everything was good. Only one action represented evil – the disobedient act of eating the forbidden fruit. However, after she ate the fruit, she became a sinner and her life became very complex and confusing. With her twisted conscience and powerful sinful will, she faced a constant battle of self-deception. Should she follow her sinful will or listen to the Spirit of God speaking through her conscience? This is the same battle we all face every day!

I like to think of the conscience as God's internal spiritual warning system within each person. We are born as physical and spiritual beings. Therefore, we have two warning systems – one physical and the other spiritual. Our physical warning system is our central nervous system. This complex system conducts stimuli from sensory receptors through the spinal cord to the brain. It sends messages to the body as a means to protect itself from things that might be threatening or harmful. Likewise, God has given us a spiritual warning system – the conscience. The conscience is that invisible part of the spirit of man where the Holy Spirit strives with man to protect him from things that would be threatening to the body and soul. In Genesis 6, where God gave His indictment against the wickedness in the days of Noah, God said, "My spirit shall not always strive with man..." (Genesis 6:3). The Hebrew word translated "strive" is a rare Hebrew word in the Bible, found only in one other passage – Job 19:29, where the same Hebrew word is translated "judgment." Hence, it appears this word gives us an insight into the work of the Holy Spirit to convict men of their sin. The Spirit strives with man in a sense of judgment of right and wrong in their conscience. In other words, our conscience is an internal judge that is passing judgment upon our thoughts, motives, and actions.

What a wonderful gift the conscience is. It is a testimony of God's unique love for mankind. Our holy God hates sin and He has given us an internal judge to guide us away from death in sin and toward life in Him. As God told Israel long ago, "I have set before you life and death, blessing and cursing: therefore choose life, that both thou and thy seed may live. That thou mayest love the LORD thy God, and that thou mayest obey his voice, and that thou mayest cleave unto him: for he is thy life" (Deuteronomy 30:19-20).

The understanding of how the conscience works is clearly spelled out by the apostle Paul in Romans 2. In this chapter, Paul brings all humanity into God's courtroom to produce the evidence that "all have sinned, and come short of the glory of God" (Romans 3:23). As Paul brings human offenders into God's courtroom, he distinguishes between the Jews who have the written law of God [Scripture] and the Gentiles who do not have the written law of God. Paul states that the Gentiles are not excused from this verdict because they show "the work of the law written in their hearts, their conscience the mean while accusing or else excusing one another" (Romans 2:15). Here, Paul describes what happens when a person is considering a thought, word, or action. If a consideration is pleasing to God, a person's good conscience will "excuse" him from guilt. However, if a consideration is offensive to God, his conscience will "accuse" or convict him it is wrong. In 1 John 3:19-20, the apostle John used two different words to describe the work of the Holy Spirit in the conscience of man. If our thoughts are good, our heart [conscience] will "assure" us what we are doing is pleasing to God. However, if our thoughts are evil, our conscience will "condemn" us. In essence, the Bible teaches that when our conscience accuses or condemns us it produces guilt, shame, anguish, regret, anxiety, disgrace, and fear. When our conscience assures or excuses us, it produces joy, peace, or a calm confidence of the work of the Spirit in us. If we are all honest, we are very familiar with this process we face every day, and all day long.

The word "strive" in Genesis 6:3 is the perfect word picture of the work of God's grace in our hearts. God loves us and is patient toward us "not willing that any should perish, but that all should come to repentance" (1 Peter 3:9). Christ died "for the sins of the whole world" (1 John 2:2). God has sent His Holy Spirit to work in our conscience to bring conviction of sin and to draw us to salvation in Christ. Without this work, no one can be saved. "No man can say that Jesus is the Lord, but by the Holy Spirit" (1 Corinthians 12:3). No one has ever been saved without the work of the Holy Spirit striving in their conscience to bring them to Christ. There are none who are seeking God (Romans 3:11). God is the one who is pursuing them (Luke 19:10).

One day while I was studying all of this, my wife asked me to go to Walmart with her. At first, I thought about saying no, but I said yes. When we arrived at the parking lot, I remembered I needed to call our son. I told my wife to go ahead of me and I would join her inside after I had talked with our son. As I finished talking with him, an unusual development took place right in front of me. A car pulled in front of my car. Inside the car was a young man who appeared to be about ten years older than the young teen girl with him. As soon as that car came to a stop, another car with a middle-aged woman quickly pulled up beside them. The woman got out of her car and reached inside of the open window of the passenger side of the car where the young girl was. It became apparent that this was a mother and daughter conflict taking place. The mom said to her daughter, "Come with me, I do not want you to be with him. He is not good for you." The daughter replied: "No Mom, I am not going with you. I am staying with him." The mother began to pull on the arm of her daughter in the car. The daughter began to scream at her mom to leave them alone. Then the mother got back in her car and called the police on her cell phone.

When the police answered, the Mom pleaded: "I am here in the parking lot at Walmart, and my daughter is a minor and is in the car with a good-for-nothing older man who is involved with drugs. I need your help now!" After hanging up, the man, who had not said a word or even made eye contact with the girl or mom, told the girl to get out and go with her mom. Apparently, he did not want the police showing up to find him with drugs. So, the girl relented and reluctantly got in the car with her mom. As they turned out of the parking lot, I saw the man in his car following them out of the parking lot and down the road. Something down deep inside of me told me this was not the end of this conflict.

As I sat there, it dawned on me that the Lord had just given me a real picture of the Holy Spirit's striving in a sinner's heart to rescue them from sin. Being a parent myself, I will never forget the desperate pleas of this mother to rescue her daughter from the grasp of this older man who obviously had ill intent. The mother's pleading voice was filled with deep emotion. She loved her daughter. She knew she was in danger. She was moved to rescue her because she cared about her and her future.

My friend, the same can be said about God. We cannot begin to fathom the love that He has for all those who have been created in His image. He cares for us. The Father cared so much that He sent His Son to suffer and die on a cruel cross for our sins. Do you know that God has emotions? The Bible says He grieves when we sin (Ephesians 4:30). Just like that mother, the Holy Spirit strives with all of us because He knows the consequences of sin. He cares about us. He does not want us to perish without God. We have been created to have a personal relationship with a holy God. God said to His own people, Israel, "As I live, saith the Lord GOD, I have no pleasure in the death of the wicked; but that the wicked turn from his way, and live: turn ye, turn ye from your evil ways; for why will ye die, O house of Israel" (Ezekiel 33:11)?

It should be abundantly clear that all of us should desire to have a strong, healthy, and functioning conscience. In the Hebrew mindset, the "heart" of man was equivalent to the conscience. Proverbs 4:23 admonishes us, "Keep thy heart [conscience] with all diligence; for out of it are the issues of life." The very stuff that life is made of – blessing and cursing, or victory and defeat – are directly linked to our conscience. The Hebrew word for "keep' in this verse was used in ancient days to refer to guarding something that was very precious. The words "with all diligence" indicate this precious gift was to be guarded more than anything else. Why? Because out of the conscience are the issues of life. The Hebrew word "issues" referred to the boundaries of a territory or city. Thus, we should guard our conscience more than anything else because it is the map or path to life. In 1 Timothy 1:5 Paul reminded his young son in the faith that having "a good conscience" was at the heart of our obedience to God.

I find it quite odd and tragic that little is being said in churches or written in Christian books and literature about the biblical view of the conscience. And yet, it is so vital in our understanding of how to walk with God and live for Christ. I believe this is possibly one of the best-kept secrets to living the Christian life. I admonish you to think and pray about what you are learning about your conscience.

In the next few chapters, we will discover what makes the conscience weak, while outlining some important steps to make it strong. I hope you will join me in discovering these important, vibrant, relevant, and life-changing truths. Our lives and our eternal destiny depend upon it!

If we really understand that people all around us in this culture are silencing their conscience, it should give us a greater passion to share the gospel with them. We need to warn them of the very sins that are destroying their conscience, while eventually leading them to eternal damnation. Like God, we need to strive with them over their souls. We need to strive in fervent prayer. We need to strive in providing them with a godly example to follow. We need to strive with them by sharing with them the saving Word of God. We need to strive with them because we love them and we care about them.

Time is of the essence. With every passing day, peoples' consciences are getting dangerously close to the point where they will be completely silenced. Then, as Romans 1 repeatedly warns, God will give them up. When God stops pursuing them, it is over! They are hopelessly and eternally lost. Remember what Jesus said? "I must work the works of him that sent me, while it is day, the night is coming, when no man can work" (John 9:4). When a person reaches the point where their conscience is silenced, they become unredeemable because the Holy Spirit has no conscience in which to strive. This makes it impossible for the Spirit to convict them of sin and bring them to salvation. Obviously, only God knows when a person reaches this hopeless point of no return.

CHAPTER 3

What Influences the Conscience?

"Keep thy heart [conscience] with all diligence:
for out of it are the issues of life."
Proverbs 4:23

I N THE PREVIOUS CHAPTER, I EXPLAINED THAT MAN'S conscience should be viewed as a spiritual warning system everyone receives at birth. People are not born with a perfect conscience. Man's original conscience, which was founded upon his understanding of the person of God and His perfect laws, was marred when the fall of man occurred in the Garden of Eden. When we are conceived, we receive our spiritual DNA, which includes a conscience that has been impacted by our sinful forefathers. The conscience is where the Holy Spirit strives with us. This work of the Holy Spirit is aimed at protecting us from sin, convicting us of our sinfulness, and ultimately bringing us into a relationship with Jesus Christ.

After birth, a person's conscience can be influenced to become stronger or weaker. What influences impact our conscience? According to the Bible, there are five influences that contribute to the strength or weakness of a person's conscience. Let us examine them.

1. Parents

The first influence that helps to form a person's conscience is the home. By God's design, parents should have the greatest influence in the life of their child. By their instructions and examples, it is a known fact that a child at an early age will mimic their parents, making their instructions and actions vitally important. The greatest responsibility of a parent is to communicate and illustrate with their lives the truths that will strengthen the conscience of their child. This vital role of parents will equip their children and protect them for the rest of their lives (Deuteronomy 6:1-7; Ephesians 6:4). In response to this parental guidance, the Bible commands children to honor and obey their parents (Ephesians 6:1-3). Proverbs 6:21-22 gives the following admonition to a child, "My son, keep thy father's commandment, and forsake not the law of thy mother. Bind them continually upon thine heart [conscience], and tie them about thy neck. When thou goest it shall lead thee; when thou sleepest, it shall keep thee; and when thou awakest, it shall talk with thee." At the heart of God's instructions to the Jewish people was the command to internalize the Word of God and to teach it to their children. In the holiest portion of Scripture for the Jewish people, God said, "And these words, which I command thee this day, shall be in thine heart: And thou shalt teach them diligently unto thy children, and shalt talk of them when thou sittest in thy house, and when thou walkest by the way, and when thou liest down, and when thou risest up" (Deuteronomy 6:6-7).

I have had the privilege of traveling to Israel numerous times. In my relationships with Jewish people I have discovered there is a great bond between children and their parents. Most Jewish parents consider their role of instilling their values in the lives of their children to be a top priority. A majority of Jewish children are told at an early age they are to live their lives in a manner that will make their homes, communities and world a better place to live. In essence, life is not just about pleasing self. Each Friday night, Jewish families gather around the Shabbat table and connect with each other. This plays a large role in the success of the Jewish people and the nation of Israel.

God designed the family to be the foundation of society. Therefore, the collapse of the family environment in our homes is one of the greatest contributing factors to the violence and wickedness that pervade our culture. Parents are too preoccupied with things other than their children. Above all things, God has entrusted our children to us as a precious gift. He expects us to make a life-time commitment to their spiritual welfare. God says, "Train up a child in the way he should go: and when he is old, he will not depart from it" (Proverbs 22:6). According to U.S. Census Bureau statics from 2017, there are an estimated twelve million single-parent families in the U.S. with children under the age of eighteen. Even more startling is the fact that the Census Bureau says that more than eighty percent of these families are headed by single mothers. This has a very detrimental impact on our society because statistics further indicate that a major contributing factor in the lives of persons who are incarcerated in the jails and prisons is the absence of a father in the home. A great number of individuals in our prison systems come from broken or dysfunctional homes. In essence, these people committed crimes against humanity because their conscience was not strengthened by the good example and instruction of a caring father. Because of their weak conscience, they had little or no moral restraint in their formative years to aid them in refraining from the crime they would commit later in life.

Parents must place an extremely high value on instructing their children to attain high moral values that flow out of the very character and nature of the God who is revealed in the Bible. Parents should ask themselves: "Do I place a high value on the souls of my children?" It appears that some parents spend more time with their child in sports or academic pursuits, while ignoring the need to feed their soul (conscience). Which is most important? Which of these will prepare them for life? Which will last for eternity? Perhaps all parents should think about their children and consider the thought-provoking question that Jesus gave to those following Him. "For what is a man profited, if he shall gain the whole world, and lose his own soul? Or what shall a man give in exchange for his soul?" (Matthew 16:26)

What kind of values are we passing along to our kids? We ask them if they have completed their homework. We ask them if they have brushed their teeth. But, do we ask them if they have had their devotions or quiet time with God? What we demand of our children certainly signals to them what we think is most important in life. What kind of signals are we sending to them about what is most important in life? Are good grades or a college degree more important than where our children will spend eternity? Is it wise to sacrifice family time and time in the Bible so our children can pursue playing some sport that will mean nothing in just a few years? Is it wise to be more concerned about the condition of their teeth than the condition of their soul or conscience? I am a living testimony that a person can be influenced by the guidance of a godly father.

Parents must not only feed their child's mind the Word of God, but they must also be diligent to guard their child's mind from influences that are not pleasing to Him. Parents must diligently monitor their children's friends, music, education, and entertainment (television, movies, computer games, etc.). Everything that passes through the gates of the eyes and ears into the mind of your child will influence their conscience. We must learn to say, "no," even if everyone else is doing it. This is why parents are called "guardians."

The collapse of the home in America is the greatest single cause for the violence and wickedness that is exploding on the streets in America. Dads and moms have not been present to guard and feed the conscience of their children. They have turned them over to our godless culture.

2. The Culture

Culture is the second influence that impacts a person's conscience. What a person thinks about everything and everyone around him influences his conscience. This is why Proverbs 4:23-27 commands us to guard what goes into our conscience. All that we hear, see, and feel will impact our conscience. Choosing the right friends is critical. The Holy Spirit selected the message of Psalm 1 as the opening chapter in the biblical collection of Psalms. Notice how it begins, "Blessed is the man that walketh not in the counsel of the ungodly, nor standeth in the way of sinners, nor sitteth in the seat of the scornful" (Psalm 1:1). Proverbs 1:10 adds, "My son, if sinners entice thee, consent thou not." We have a tendency to value the opinions of those we choose to spend time with. A person will be happy in his relationship with God and his conscience when he selects good influences. Proverbs 23:7 says, "For as he thinketh in his heart, so is he." We become what we think, and our thinking is guided by our conscience.

A person must make right choices about what he will embrace in his culture. This includes friends, educational institutions, entertainment choices, music choices, reading material, recreational opportunities, etc. In essence, a person must guard his conscience from anything that will influence him in a direction away from God and His Word. In our present American culture this has become extremely difficult! We live in a culture that hates God and is in defiant rebellion against Him and His Word. We live at a time when people in our culture celebrate the very things that destroy the conscience. Our children and teens have godless and wicked idols and heroes.

I am a traveling evangelist. When I am invited to speak at a church for several days, I occasionally stay with the pastor and his family in their home. Years ago, I shall never forget, the pastor of the host church chose for me to stay in his son's bedroom. His son was only ten years old. When I got into his bedroom I was stunned and shocked. The walls were covered with huge colorful posters of movie actors and rock stars. I wondered why any father would allow his son to watch or listen to anything these people would say or do. Needless to say, I had a difficult time sleeping in that room. I was sleeping in a room with posters that were glorifying people who were damning children and teens to hell with their music and lifestyles. This pastor was allowing his son to idolize people who were immoral, violent, and far away from God.

Friends, I believe we do not realize we are living in a godless, pagan culture that is far away from God. Life is not just a simple little game we are playing. As Christians, we are constantly living in a spiritual warzone. Our lives and where we will spend eternity are at stake! I have concluded, if this godless world system adores it, God is against it. Please think about James 4:4, "Ye adulterers and adulteresses, know ye not that the friendship of the world is enmity with God? Whosoever therefore will be a friend of the word is the enemy of God."

Are you in love with this world system? This present world system is wicked, sensual, arrogant, and in love with sinful pleasures. If you are attracted to this culture you are in serious trouble because you are feeding your conscience with this evil influence and it is damning your soul! The Bible declares, "Love not the world, neither the things that are in the world. If any man love the world, the love of the Father is not in him. For all that is in the world, the lust of flesh, and the lust of the eyes, and the pride of life, is not of the Father, but is of this world" (1 John 2:15-16).

3. Human Government

The third influence that impacts the conscience of a person is their government. People must submit to their government "for conscience sake" (Romans 13:5). According to the Bible, human government was created by God after the global flood to protect and defend human life. At the core of the institution of human government is capital punishment. God said, "Whoso sheddeth man's blood, by man shall his blood be shed: for in the image of God made he man" (Genesis 9:6).

God did not give human government a blank check to create its own laws. According to the Bible, all power and authority given to government comes from God (Romans 13:4). By God's design, human government should adopt and promote the moral and ethical laws of God, since human government is viewed in the Bible as an extension of God's authority on earth. Therefore, when people resist their government, they are resisting the authority of God (Romans 13:2).

Government has a powerful influence upon the conscience of its people. If people do not know God's law, they have a tendency to adopt their government's value system and laws as being acceptable. When governments become corrupt and do not promote or defend the value of human life, they are not setting the standards that reflect God's values of good and evil, right and wrong. Obviously, this will weaken the conscience of that nation.

This was illustrated in 1998 when President Bill Clinton had an affair with Monica Lewinsky. Ms. Lewinsky, who was a White House intern, performed oral sex on the president in the Oval Office. In the aftermath of these illicit actions, it was reported that the practice of oral sex rose dramatically among the youth population in the United States.

In 2015, the U.S. Supreme Court ruled that same sex unions and marriages should be honored in the same way biblical marriage has been respected in America for hundreds of years. This ruling was honored and glorified by President Barack Obama. In fact, after the Supreme Court made its ruling, the Obama White House was illuminated in rainbow colors as a nod to the achievement of the gay rights movement. Secular and biblical history demonstrates that these kinds of decisions lead to the moral corruption of a nation, destroying homes and lives in the process.

4. The Church

The word church means "called out." The church is made up of all true born-again believers who have been "called out" of this world system to be God's ambassadors on earth (2 Corinthians 5:20). With our words and actions, we are to be God's messengers. Our assignment is to reconcile the world to a holy God (2 Corinthians 5:18-19). By our lifestyles and teachings, we are to represent God so people can see God in us. We are "salt" and "light" (Matthew 5:13-14). As salt and light, we are to clearly reflect God's holiness to the world so they can see and know right from wrong and are able to identify sin and righteousness. Obviously, this is at the heart of developing a good conscience. Consequently, the church should have a restraining influence upon its culture.

When churches in a culture are faithfully proclaiming the message of the Bible to inform the conscience of their culture of God's standards of sin and righteousness, it will have a powerful impact upon that culture. We have heard many testimonies from great revivals in the past. When the fear of God moved upon a church, and God's people repented of their sins, then bars, nightclubs, and brothels had to close because many of their customers heard the gospel and were saved. Sadly, too many churches in America no longer talk about sin. In some cases, lifestyles of their members are not any different than those who never attend church. This is because the pastors and other leaders of the church are not teaching believers what God says about holiness and sin. And, in too many cases, the leadership of the church is godless and has disqualified itself from serving the body of Christ.

Too many pastors and church leaders in America are preoccupied with pleasing people. They believe they need to adapt the message of the Bible in order to not offend those who hear it. In John 15:18- 16:1, Jesus warned his disciples about this kind of thinking. He reminded them that the world hated Him because He spoke the truth and exposed people's sin, bringing conviction. Jesus' preaching directly confronted the conscience of His culture. This type of preaching is not pleasing to people. They want approval of their sinful lifestyle. When the conscience is confronted with God's holy standards, it will bring shame, guilt, and remorse. For those who are in love with their sin, this is painful and unacceptable. That is good! It is this kind of guilt that leads to repentance that brings salvation and godly change for the glory of God.

The leadership of the church in America must wake up and realize if they go soft on sin and do not point people to a holy God, they are condemning people to eternal damnation. If people's consciences are not confronted with the truth, then the conscience of that culture will become weak, driving people further away from God and His truth. When this happens, the church has become a part of the problem in that culture, rather than being a reconciler of sinful men to a holy God. Remember, the conscience is where the Holy Spirit strives with man to convict him of sin and reconcile man to God. It is my firm belief that the current wickedness and violence in America are a commentary on the failure of the church to be God's salt and light.

In the days of the prophet Jeremiah, he was hated by his own people because he confronted them with their wickedness and spoke of the imminent judgment of God upon the nation of Israel. During Jeremiah's time there were many false preachers. The same problem exists in America today. In Jeremiah 23, God condemned these false prophets because they were not proclaiming the Word of God, but spoke "a vision of their own heart, and not out of the mouth of the LORD" (Jeremiah 23:16). Notice what God said about the false prophets. "If they had stood in my counsel, and had caused my people to hear my words, then they should have turned them from their evil way, and from the evil of their doings" (Jeremiah 23:22). God placed the blame for the sinful conditions in Israel upon the failure of these false prophets to faithfully proclaim the Word of God to His people.

The basic role of the Holy Spirit in our individual lives as Christians, and collectively in the church, is to "reprove the world of sin, and of righteousness, and of judgment" (John 16:8). Once again, please understand that the reproving or convicting work of the Holy Spirit takes place in His striving in the conscience of a person. When we faithfully proclaim and live a life that clearly points to what God says about sin, righteousness, and the judgment of God, then we are cooperating with the Holy Spirit in His work to convict sinners and bring them to Christ. However, when the church ignores this message of warning from God, it contributes to the defilement of the collective conscience of that culture.

In the ancient biblical setting, warning people to prepare for danger was a vital responsibility. Many people lived in walled cities. A watchtower was built high above the wall so a watchman could scan the horizon to look for any possible threat. If a watchman failed to warn his people of danger, it usually cost him his life. Following this custom, God told the prophet Ezekiel, "Son of man, I have made thee a watchman unto the house of Israel, therefore hear the word at my mouth, and give them warning from me. When I say unto the wicked, Thou shalt surely die; and thou givest him not warning, nor speaketh to warn the wicked from his wicked way, to save his life; the same wicked man shall die in his iniquity; but his blood will I require at thy hand. Yet, if thou warn the wicked, and he turn not from his wickedness, nor from his wicked way, he shall die in his iniquity; but thou hast delivered thy soul" (Ezekiel 3:17-19). Today, believers in Jesus Christ are the watchmen on the walls of America. We must faithfully warn our fellow Americans concerning sin, righteousness, and judgment. If we fail to do this, their blood and eternal damnation will be on our hands.

5. The Bible

The perfect and most powerful influence upon the conscience of man is the Word of God. Remember that our conscience is a gift from God because we have been created in His image. The conscience is the place within our inner man where God speaks to us and attempts to rescue us from the deadly effects of sin. The Holy Spirit wants the best for us. God is a good God. Goodness is a part of who He is. He created us for a relationship with Him and to bring Him glory. The Holy Spirit is the One who reconciles men to God by convicting men of the dangers and the eternal end results of sin. He wants to convince men to surrender to God and allow Him to begin the restoration process of changing who they are. At the core of this is the restoration of a pure conscience. God's revelation about Himself is the standard from which our conscience must compare all matters of good and evil.

The Bible is the only perfect tool the Holy Spirit has at His disposal to accomplish this goal, and in the process, begin the restoration of a pure conscience. "All scripture is given by inspiration of God, and is profitable for doctrine, for reproof, for correction, for instruction in righteousness: That the man of God may be perfect, thoroughly furnished unto all good works" (2 Timothy 3:16-17). In essence, the Bible is God's perfect tool the Holy Spirit uses to strengthen the conscience of a godly man. The Bible is the powerful instrument the Holy Spirit uses to convert the soul and begin the restoration of the conscience of man. "The law of the LORD is perfect, converting the soul; the testimony of the LORD is sure, making wise the simple. The statutes of the LORD are right, rejoicing the heart [conscience]: the commandment of the LORD is pure, enlightening the eyes. The fear of the LORD is clean, enduring forever: the judgments of the LORD are true and righteous altogether. … Moreover by them is thy servant warned: and in keeping them there is great reward" (Psalm 19:7-9, 11).

The godly man who has a good conscience will be exceptionally careful to guard his conscience from evil influences and strengthen it by feeding it the Word of God. This man will be blessed by God and he will have a spiritually prosperous life. As a person reads the book of Psalms, which is dedicated to a person's personal relationship and worship of God, it begins with a significant statement. "Blessed is the man that walketh not in the counsel of the ungodly, nor standeth in the way of sinners, nor sittteth in the seat of the scornful. But his delight is in the law of the LORD, and in his law doth he meditate day and night" (Psalm 1:1-2).

The restoration of a pure conscience is the ultimate ongoing desire of the Holy Spirit, constantly directing the person to internalize the Word of God. That is why Psalm 119:11 declares, "Thy word have I hid in mine heart, that I might not sin against thee." The Bible is the most direct and perfect tool to influence the conscience. We will explore all of this in greater detail in the next chapter.

CHAPTER 4

What Makes the Conscience Weak?

"Today if ye will hear [God's] voice, harden
not your hearts [consciences]."
Hebrews 3:15

W E HAVE EXAMINED FIVE INFLUENCES OF THE
conscience. But, this does not answer the question of how
the conscience is weakened or silenced. The Bible teaches us that
sin desensitizes the conscience. When a person is considering doing
something that is offensive to God, his conscience will produce guilt
concerning that action. However, our sinful nature and its desire for
instant pleasure persuade our personal will that this is what we want. In
our craving for instant gratification, we sometimes ignore the warning of
the conscience. When this happens, it can begin the process of silencing
the conscience. As this process continues it gets easier to ignore the Holy
Spirit's striving through the conscience.

The Bible uses many different terms to express what sin does to the
conscience. Hebrews 3:15 says, "Today if ye will hear his voice, harden
not your hearts (consciences)..." When a person does not immediately
obey the work of the Holy Spirit in his conscience and chooses to disobey
God, it will harden (numb) his conscience. According to 1 Timothy
4:1-2, a person's conscience can be numbed as if it were "seared with

a hot iron." If they suppress the truth of God in their conscience and accept lies and deception, they are searing their conscience. They are making their conscience insensitive to the warnings of sin. The apostle Paul reminded the Corinthian believers that when people have a weak conscience it is easy for their conscience to be "defiled" (1 Corinthians 8:7) or "wounded" (1 Corinthians 8:12).

If you are computer literate, you have probably experienced what happens when one of your computer files becomes corrupted. When that computer file is corrupted, it means that the manufactured reader on your computer is unable to read the corrupted file. Therefore, that file becomes useless and must be deleted. When our conscience is weak and does not have a strong biblical foundation, it is easy for our conscience to be further damaged or defiled.

Please keep in mind that the work of the Holy Spirit in man's conscience is the only means whereby God can restrain a person from the deadly dangers of sin. According to the Bible, a nation or individual can spiritually reach a point of no return. This means that the Lord's work of grace and restraint in their conscience ceases, and they are left to their own foolishness and ultimate eternal demise. A person or culture reaches this point when the Spirit of God can no longer do a work in the human conscience to produce a fear of evil that can lead them to repentance. When this takes place, God gives them over to their destructive ways (Romans 1:24-27). This spiritual point of no return is irreversible! John MacArthur, Jr. states in his excellent book, *The Vanishing Conscience*, "Obliterate the human conscience, and you will raise an amoral and unredeemable generation." [1]

When this takes place, another horrific spiritual tragedy takes place. When a person no longer has a functioning conscience and is completely driven by his sinful rebellion against God, he will be open to demonic oppression or possession. The Bible informs us that demons, who are fallen angels (see Revelation 9:11), roam the earth looking for individuals to enslave. Simply stated, they are looking for a person who will become their puppet. They want a person whose conscience has been seared. This person will have no inhibitions. Therefore, the demons will be able to use that person's body and mind to accomplish their hellish agenda while destroying their victim at the same time. 1 Timothy 4:1-2 gives the following warning about the end of this age, "Now the Spirit speaketh expressly, that in the latter times some shall depart from the faith, giving heed to seducing spirits and doctrines of [demons]: Speaking lies in hypocrisy; having their conscience seared with a hot iron."

When people have no conscience and they are influenced by demons, they will act like animals. They will be filled with a spirit of lawlessness, greed, violence, murder, hatred, immorality, and arrogance. (Read the complete list in Romans 1:29-31.) They will exhibit unmerciful behavior, while also being unloving and unthankful. Moreover, they will be fierce, lack self-control, and have a deep passion for sinful pleasure. A person influenced by demons will hate God and all of those who want to be like God. (Read the complete list in 2 Timothy 3:2-5.) If we are honest, we must admit this is a description of the current American culture. In chapter eleven we will examine the kind of culture in which demons flourish in their quest to control a society.

Sadly, the reality of demons and hell is not being taught in our so-called evangelical churches today. And while churches tragically neglect their duties, the Bible says the future of a nation depends upon the good conscience of its citizens. This creates the foundation upon which a nation lives and works. If that foundation is weakened or destroyed, the nation will be destroyed also. "If the foundations be destroyed, what can the righteous do?" (Psalm 11:3)

CHAPTER 5

What Makes the Conscience Strong?

"Thy word have I hid in mine heart [conscience],
that I might not sin against [God]."
Psalm 119:11

ACCORDING TO THE BIBLE, WE SHOULD STRIVE DAILY to have a pure (good) conscience (1 Timothy 1:5 and 3:9). A good example of this is found in the life of King Josiah of Judah in the Old Testament. He came to reign in Jerusalem when he was only eight years old. Then, at the age of sixteen, he began to seek after the God of David. The Bible reports that King Josiah reigned in Jerusalem for thirty-one years. "And he did that which was right in the sight of the LORD, and walked in the ways of David his father, and declined neither to the right hand, nor to the left" (2 Chronicles 34:2). God blessed King Josiah because his "heart [conscience] was tender" (2 Chronicles 34:27). This means that the king had an extremely sensitive conscience. When King Josiah considered a matter, his conscience was so sensitive it immediately caused him to fear or have a deep reverence for God. If he thought about sinning, his heart was flooded with anxiety, shame and guilt. When Josiah considered doing what was right in the sight of God, his conscience overflowed with confidence, peace and assurance.

King David's life and testimony, recorded in the psalms he wrote, also give us great insight to what happens when a godly person who has a strong conscience sins against God. When David was a young shepherd boy caring for his father's sheep, he knew God and developed a strong personal relationship with Him. In Psalm 23, he referred to God as "my shepherd" (verse 1) and spoke about how God restored his soul and led him "in the paths of righteousness for his name's sake" (verse 3). Later in his life, he became the powerful king of Israel and sinned against God by committing adultery and murder. Under the guidance of the Holy Spirit, David later wrote about his experience of trying to ignore his sin. According to Psalm 32 and 51, David attempted to ignore the striving of the Holy Spirit in his conscience for a period of time. For a while, David refused to yield to the striving of the Holy Spirit in his conscience. He described how his conscience pursued him. "When I kept silence, my bones waxed old through my roaring all the day long. For day and night thy hand was heavy upon me: my moisture is turned into the drought of summer" (Psalm 32:3, 4). In Psalm 51:3 he exclaimed, "My sin is ever before me." In these verses, David was describing the anxiety, guilt, and anguish that gnawed at his inner soul as his conscience continually strived with him until he confessed his sin to God. King David described how he was restored to the sweet fellowship and joy that comes when a person obeys God's work in his conscience.

After David confessed his sin, he realized his struggle was not over. He had been forgiven, but his conscience had been defiled. With confession, God removes the guilt of sin, but this does not heal the damage that sin has inflicted upon the conscience. David's wounded conscience needed to be repaired. Therefore, he prayed, "Create in me a clean heart [conscience], O God: and renew a right spirit within me" (Psalm 51:10).

The majority of Christians do not understand the impact that sin has on weakening their conscience. Most Christians believe that when they have sinned, all they need to do is confess their sin and it, and the accompanying guilt, will all go away. It is true that "if we confess our sins, he is faithful and just to forgive our sins, and to cleanse us from all unrighteousness" (1 John 1:9). We are truly forgiven, but that does not heal the conscience or erase the consequences of our sin. To illustrate, consider this. If a man has smoked a pack of cigarettes each day for 25 years and he is suddenly convicted and confesses his sin, he is immediately forgiven for smoking. However, this does not cleanse his lungs from the effects of smoking. After God has forgiven him, he must continue to suffer the consequences of his 25-year addiction. The Bible says, "Be not deceived, God is not mocked: for whatsoever a man soweth, that shall he also reap. For he that soweth to his flesh shall of the flesh reap corruption: but he that soweth to the Spirit shall of the Spirit reap life everlasting" (Galatians 6:7-8).

After a person has confessed any sin, he must remember that he must strengthen his conscience if he is to have victory over the power of sin. All sin is addictive! Sin is a cruel slave master. It is like cancer. It sinks its deadly roots deep into the conscience of its victim. Victory begins by turning it over to Jesus. "If the Son therefore shall make you free, ye shall be free indeed" (John 8:36). However, as mentioned above, Jesus does forgive us and give us the strength to be set free. The ultimate victory over the deadliness of sin is to internalize the Word of God and apply it to the particular area of the struggle. "And ye shall know the truth, and the truth shall make you free" (John 8:32).

All too often, Christians struggle with the same sin and keep confessing it over and over again. They need to understand the power of sin. Christian author and apologist Ravi Zacharias has said: "Sin will take you farther than you want to go. Sin will keep you longer that you want to stay. And, sin will make you pay far more than you want to pay!" Clearly, victory comes when we pursue a pure conscience. We must do it God's way!

Real victory over any sin begins with genuine repentance and confession. However, to really have the victory, this must be followed up with the pursuit of a pure conscience. As children of God, we should desire a sensitive conscience. We should desire to be quickly filled with the fear of God when sin presents itself to us. As a Christian, I want a conscience that screams out at me with shame and guilt when I just think about doing something that is displeasing to God. That is a strong conscience.

A god-pleasing conscience is the result of one's childhood upbringing with godly parents. It comes when a person does not allow human government, the culture, or flaws in the doctrine and practice of the church to lead them astray. Most important of all, the person must commit to internalizing the Word of God. Remember Psalm 119:11, "Thy word have I hid in mine heart [conscience] that I might not sin against thee." I believe that many Christians quote this verse, but do not know how to put it into practice in their daily lives.

Let me share a personal story from my life as a pastor that will help illustrate how we are to put Psalm 119:11 into practice to strengthen our conscience. Many years ago, when I was a pastor in a church in a rural community, the phone rang in my office. The call was one of my elderly church members. To protect their identity I will call them Bob and Mary. Mary was crying and asked if I could come to help her and Bob with something that was destroying their relationship and marriage. I immediately left my office and drove to their home, which was about 5 minutes away. This elderly couple lived on a farm and they had only been married a few years. Both of them attended my church on a regular basis. I really felt like I had a very good relationship with both of them.

When I entered their home, Bob and Mary were sitting beside each other on the couch, and were weeping. I will never forget this experience. When I asked what the problem was, Bob began to sob and explained that prior to Mary's call he had lashed out at her and said some extremely hurtful things. He said, "Pastor, please help me, I have a quick temper that leads me to say things that I immediately regret when my anger begins to cool down. I have had a problem with uncontrollable anger all my life. Please help me. I will do anything you tell me. I do not want to live like this anymore."

I did not hesitate to give him an answer. I knew what he needed to do. I asked: "Are you really willing to do anything that God tells you to do to get your temper under control?" Bob said, "Yes, I will do anything!"

I asked them if they had a Bible concordance. They said they did not even know what that was. I explained that a Bible concordance was a book that listed words in the Bible and the verses where that particular word is found throughout the Bible. I told them I would go to the church and I return in a few minutes with the spiritual prescription to help him control his anger. I went to the office and copied all of the pages in the Bible concordance that listed the words connected to anger, malice, and wrath. Upon returning to their home, I showed these pages to Bob and told him what I wanted him to do. I asked him to read all of these verses in the Bible about anger. (There were hundreds of them.) I told him this assignment would take several months, but if he was serious about controlling his anger, God could help him. But, he had to do it God's way.

I further explained that as he was reading these verses, they would really speak to his heart about his anger. I advised him that as he came across some of these verses he wanted to remember, he needed to write each one down along with the Bible reference on a small piece of paper. I further advised him to place these pieces of paper in his shirt pocket and to read only one verse at a time for several days. I told him to read each verse while he was shaving in the morning. I asked him to read it when he was relaxing in his chair during the day. I challenged him to read it when he came to a stop light and was waiting for the light to change. I requested that he read that verse as he was doing his chores around the farm. Basically, I asked him to read, reread, and meditate upon that verse. I explained that the goal was for that verse to be internalized in his conscience so that when the temptation to blow his cool would come, the Holy Spirit could point him to these verses and give him power to refrain from losing his temper. I informed him that if he would do this with many of the verses, I could guarantee that God would help him with his temper. After a time of prayer, I left and went back to the office.

About eight months later, my phone in the office rang and again it was the same dear lady who had called me before. Mary said, "Pastor, Bob and I would like to invite you to come to our house and have lunch with us." I never turned down an invitation like that. I also wanted to check up on the assignment I gave to the husband. When I entered their home they both met me at the door with smiles and gave me a big hug. As we sat down to eat lunch, Mary said: "Thanks to the Bible, I have a new husband. He has not said a harsh word to me since you were here before." Bob thanked me for helping him. He shared how he followed through with what I had told him to do. He said: "Pastor, for the first time in my life, I have been able to control my temper. The Bible works!"

The Bible always works. It is God's word. I have used this principle in my counseling for decades to explain that anyone who has obeyed the Bible has victory. When a person saturates his conscience with Bible verses that deal with his sin problem, the Holy Spirit will help him develop a strong conscience so that when temptation comes, the conscience is equipped to give him victory.

The believer must saturate his conscience with the Word of God. His goal should be to teach his conscience the standard of Biblical reality in three areas.

First, he needs to have a biblical perception of God. He needs to know who God is. He needs to focus on what the Bible says about the attributes of God. Proverbs 16:6 says, "By the fear of the LORD men depart from evil." Proverbs 9:10 declares, "The fear of the LORD is the beginning of wisdom: and the knowledge of the holy [One] gives understanding." These two verses, and many others like them, teach us that the knowledge of God is the foundation and starting point to having victory over sin. Why? That which is right and wholesome for the mind and soul of a person is bound up in the nature of God. God's nature defines what is good, righteous, just, and pure. To know God is to know what is right and good. This is why God's standard of right and wrong never changes. God never changes! Therefore, His standard of right and wrong never changes!

Secondly, the believer needs to focus upon is his own total depravity. When you look at who God is and learn that He is holy and pure, you will discover that you are not a good person. When the prophet Isaiah was caught up into God's throne room in heaven in Isaiah 6 he was awed by the holiness of God. Then, he said, "Woe is me! For I am undone;

because I am a man of unclean lips, and I dwell in the midst of a people of unclean lips: for mine eyes have seen the King, the LORD of hosts" (Isaiah 6:5). If we fail to see God as being holy, then we will fail to see that we are desperately sinful. The more you are in awe of God's holiness, the more you will be horrified by your sinfulness! Jeremiah grasped this when he wrote: "The heart is deceitful above all things and desperately wicked" (Jeremiah 17:9). The apostle Paul testified, "For I know that in me (that is in my flesh), [dwells] no good thing …. O wretched man that I am" (Romans 7:18, 24)!

Educating our conscience concerning our total depravity is extremely valuable. We must try to grasp how desperately dependent we are upon God and His truth. His Word and His ways are infinitely higher than our thoughts (Isaiah 55:6-11)! We can think we are right, when in reality we are deceived and are deadly wrong. We must learn to never trust ourselves or others. We must only trust God. Jesus put it plainly, "Without me ye can do nothing" (John 15:5).

The third standard of biblical reality with which we need to fill our conscience is the deceitfulness of sin. Our conscience is "hardened through the deceitfulness of sin" (Hebrews 3:13). Our minds and souls must be filled with the raw biblical reality of the awfulness and deadliness of sin. "All sin is gross, disgusting, loathsome and revolting in God's sight. Sin is called 'filthiness' (Prov. 30:12; Ezek. 24:13; Jas. 1:21). Sin is compared to vomit, and sinners are the dogs that lick it up (Prov. 26:11; 2 Pet. 2:22). Sin is called mire, and sinners are the swine who love to wallow in it (Ps. 69:2; 2 Pet. 2:22). Sin is likened to a putrefying corpse, and sinners are the tombs that continue the stench and foulness (Matt. 23:37). Sin has turned humanity into a polluted, befouled race." [1]

We must never go soft on sin. We must educate our conscience concerning the nature and consequences of sin. Our conscience must be constantly informed of the many biblical warnings concerning all sin. We should pray that our conscience would be flooded with a fear of the consequences of sin. All sin is deadly and destructive. It grieves God and breaks our fellowship with Him. It destroys relationships! It defiles the conscience, poisons the mind, inflicts the body, and ultimately brings death. Sin begins with what appears to be a fleeting, pleasurable moment of lust. However, we must remember, "When lust hath conceived, it bringeth forth sin, and sin, when it is finished, bringeth forth death" (James 1:15).

CHAPTER 6

Living in a Nation of Fools

"When they knew God, they glorified him not as God, neither
were thankful; but became vain in their imaginations,
their foolish [conscience] was darkened. Professing
themselves to be wise, they became fools."
Romans 1:22

WHEN THE COLLECTIVE CONSCIENCE OF A CULTURE
has been silenced, people make choices without a moral/
intellectual compass. Common sense ceases to exist. They may
be academically brilliant, but their self-guided passion for instant
gratification causes them to make foolish choices. They become slaves
to emotional and physical indulgence. They are so driven by their quest
for pleasure they become blind to their deadly choices.

We live in a nation and a world that are hurtling down a path
that is clearly marked "Destruction Ahead." The majority of people are
ignoring the few godly voices of warning that are declaring that danger
lies just ahead. These people do not know it, but they are living the life
of a person the Bible calls "a fool." We need to spiritually shout out to
these people, "Turn back!"

I have asked myself in recent years, "Has the world gone mad?" The
path that many Americans have chosen does not seem to make any

sense to me. It is foolish! It is dangerous! And, it is deadly! People really do not seem to care about their choices or their lifestyles. It seems they are totally oblivious to the fact that they are one heartbeat away from eternal damnation.

We live in a world of madness where we kill innocent unborn babies in the name of convenience. Some people are so confused they claim they do not know if they are a male or a female. Some are intoxicated with their wicked pleasures, ignoring the reality they are destroying their soul, body, mind, marriage and family. I believe we are witnessing the beginning of a horrific financial collapse as the madness to gratify self is driving people into financial bondage, creating a tremendous bubble of debt that will soon explode in the face of all Americans. We live in an hour of such foolishness when many are crying out for freedom from the laws of God and man. They want to be free to express the lawlessness of their depraved heart in rebellion against God, government, our nation, and their family. Their way is the only way. But, according to the Bible, their way is not only wrong, but deadly. And, it is not only deadly to them, but to those who daily or casually cross their path of destruction.

I can hear some of you say, "This is not new. All of this foolishness has been going on for a very long time." You are right! All of this has happened before. A study of biblical and extra-biblical history clearly demonstrates that the preceding generations, all the way back to the Genesis flood, repeated this cycle of madness. I have had the privilege of walking among the remains of many of these ancient civilizations in the Middle East. What they left behind gives silent testimony to the foolishness that brought about their ultimate demise. However, in light of the overall context of our world, according to prophetic Scripture, I am convinced we are about to witness the final act of madness that will invite God's final retribution upon all of mankind. I am absolutely convinced this is man's last defiant rebellion against God and His truth.

I believe the average American church needs to wake up! Instead of shining the light of God's truth into this dark madness, too many churches have followed the world and its path of foolishness. If we are to rescue fools from their depraved madness and ultimate destruction, believers must stop acting like fools and be wise. Church ministries to children and youth must stop teaching our kids to be fools by appealing to their pleasures, instead of training them to be holy disciples of Christ.

In order to understand this, we must examine what the Bible says about "the fool." When a person or culture has reached the point of self-destruction, they are playing the part of the biblical fool. Let us examine the biblical description of a fool.

The word "fool" appears 110 times in the Bible. There are six different Hebrew words and six different Greek words translated "fool." This illustrates that the biblical message concerning the fool is remarkably detailed and must be taken seriously.

According to the Bible, the fool is not just a silly person. The fool is not someone who lacks intellectual knowledge. The fool is not someone to tease. He is a person we must warn and for whom we must pray. The fool's only hope is in Jesus Christ. The fool is enslaved to his pride-filled, sinful heart. Only Jesus can set him free so that he may make wise choices that will glorify God and be eternally healthy for his own soul. As we shall see, the person who lives the lifestyle of a fool is not saved. We may all act foolishly at times, but, the one who is constantly living the lifestyle of a fool has never been saved.

According to the Bible, the fool has three core sins:

1. He Spurns God

All fools reject God. Some refuse to acknowledge that God even exists. "The fool hath said in his heart, There is no God..." (Psalm 14:1). The word "fool" in this text is the Hebrew word "nabal," which speaks of "moral perversity." In essence, the Bible declares the fool does not want to admit there is a God because he is in love with his sin. He realizes that if he acknowledges the God of the Bible, he will be accountable to Him. Psalm 10:4 declares, "The wicked, through the pride of his countenance, will not seek after God; God is not in all his thoughts."

Some fools intellectually believe in God. However, they rarely acknowledge God's power or presence in their world. They are not intellectual fools; but they are practical fools. Professing believers are biblically admonished not to live like these practical fools (Proverbs 3:5-6).

When a nation begins to collectively reject God and fails to respond to the warning of their conscience, it becomes a nation of fools and consequently abandons its spiritual compass. As a result, great confusion sets in. The people stumble about in spiritual and mental darkness. Their lives are filled with moral, financial, marital and spiritual failure. Their conscience is "darkened." (Romans 1:21) And, they lack common sense. Their spiritual compass is broken and they cannot solve their problems or find solutions.

It is painfully obvious that America is rejecting God. We no longer are a "Christian" nation. Like those whom God has given up, they no longer want to "retain God in their knowledge" (Romans 1:28). Some of these blind fools may claim they love a god, but they really are "haters of [the] God" (Romans 1:30). They have created a god and a Jesus that fits their desires and lifestyles. But their god is not the God of the Bible. When faced with the truth about the biblical God and His truth, they not only rebel against Him, but they also adopt a lifestyle that is defiant and filled with hatred against Him, His Word, and His people.

America is in the midst of a godless revival. We have become a pagan nation. Wickedness, immorality, deception, and violence are growing and spreading across the nation like a raging wildfire. It is destroying the lives of many fools and their innocent families and friends. It is both painful and frightening to watch!

There is really only one message that must be delivered: "Turn back! Repent! You are heading down the path of destruction!" Proverbs 14:27 says, "The fear of the LORD is a fountain of life..." The path to God is paved with life, not death. God commands people choose life, not death. Listen to God's invitation, "Now therefore hearken unto me, O ye children: for blessed are they that keep my ways. Hear instruction, and be wise, and refuse it not. ... For whoso findeth me findeth life, and shall obtain favor of the LORD. But he that sinneth against me wrongeth his own soul: all they that hate me love death" (Proverbs 8:32-33, 35-36).

When fools turn away from God, it may feel right to their depraved, pride-filled minds. However, this is utter insanity! How and why should a person turn away from the God who sent His Son to die for them? He is the God who made them and sustains their life. He is the God who has given them all good things to enjoy. He is the One who created it all and controls it all. Only a fool turns away from a loving and caring God like this!

2. He Suppresses the Truth

When a person rejects God, it is only logical that he will also reject His Word – the Bible. In Romans 1, those who reject God and have become fools also suppress "the truth in unrighteousness" (Romans 1:18). A fool primarily rejects biblical truth because it is bound up in the very nature and character of God. He knows that if he accepts God's Word, he is acknowledging God and is accepting His authority. This is not what he wants. He wants to remain independent of God and His Word. The foolish man loves his lifestyle of sin and is not willing to surrender it to follow Christ. He is very comfortable being a fool because he feels that he is right. His sinful nature gives it a stamp of approval and that is all that matters to him.

God and His Word are intricately woven together. Jesus said, "I am the way, the truth, and the life: no man cometh unto the Father, but by me" (John 14:6). Like God, His Word is perfect, powerful and eternal. The wisdom of this world falls woefully short of the wisdom of God. 1 Corinthians 3:19 states, "For the wisdom of this world is foolishness with God..." God's Word is so infinite that the unsaved man cannot understand it. It is foolishness to him. The Bible says, "the natural man receiveth not the things of the Spirit of God: for they are foolishness unto him, neither can he know them, because they are spiritually discerned" (1 Corinthians 2:14).

One of the chief trademarks of a fool is his rejection of truth or counseling. Proverbs 1:7 declares, "...fools despise wisdom and instruction." Proverbs 1:22 adds, "fools hate knowledge." Have you ever met a person who had his mind already made up? No matter what you said, or what truth you presented to him, it was rejected because he knows he is right. This is the way a fool thinks. He is close minded. "The way of a fool is right in his own eyes" (Proverbs 12:15).

Those of us who walk in the light of God's truth look at fools and we are bewildered by their actions and lifestyles. The path of life looks so clear to us, but at the same time it is so oblivious to them. That is because the sinner is spiritually dead. He is walking in spiritual darkness. As children of God, we have been called "out of darkness into [Christ's marvelous] light" (1 Peter 2:9).

Because man has been created in the image of God, he possesses a conscience and common sense. While we cannot pretend to understand how they function together, it is apparent that the conscience and common sense are almost identical to each other. David Kupelain, an award-winning journalist, vice president and managing editor of World Net Daily, editor of *Whistleblower* magazine, and author of *The Marketing of Evil, How Evil Works, and The Snapping of the American Mind*, states that common sense "is the mysterious essence of logic, clear-thinking, right acting, and as such is a priceless gift from the Creator. It is the twin brother of conscience, the heartbeat of a competent, successful life."[1]

God has placed a basic sense of His law in the conscience of every person (Romans 1:19; 2:14-15). This inner spiritual warning system was twisted and distorted by the fall of man. However, the simple revelation of God in the conscience and creation still functions at some level, so that the unbeliever is "without excuse" (Romans 1:20). Some cultures have a long history of being saturated with biblical preaching. So, they have clearly been impacted with the light of God's revelation. But sadly, most cultures remained shrouded in spiritual darkness. However, in some cases, these godless cultures maintain a simple level of respect for God and His laws. It is through this respect for God and His law that the Holy Spirit prepares the hearts of the sinners in that culture to receive the gospel.

When we look back a few hundred years at the history of our great nation, it is evident that it was founded by godly pilgrims who came to this land to worship and serve their God. They left behind a very powerful legacy of their faith. Their biblical faith and proclamation of God's truth settled upon the hearts of unbelievers, like the framers of our constitution. Some of the signers of the U.S. Constitution were born-again believers, while others were not. However, by their own testimony, some of the non-believers apparently had a sense of respect for God and His Word. This respect for God and His Word was reflected in the wording of the constitution and it has continued to impact our nation for quite a long time. Nevertheless, it is apparent this residual cultural respect for God and His Word has almost completely dissipated. The impact of the early American pilgrims as salt and light is quickly disappearing. We are living in an increasingly secular culture, devoid of respect for God and His Word.

This current generation of Americans is following the path of others before them. For example, compare this with Judges 2:10-11, "And also all that generation were gathered unto their fathers: and there arose another generation after them, which knew not the LORD, nor yet the works which he had done for Israel. And the children of Israel did evil in the sight of the LORD ..." Two hundred years after the children of Israel had crossed over the Jordan and experienced the miraculous hand of God at Jericho and other battles of war, a new generation arose that had been impacted by the godless culture of the inhabitants of the land. This occurred because of disobedience, as the Israelites did not drive out the inhabitants as the Lord command them. In a similar way, this present American generation has forgotten the great price paid by the godly pilgrims who impacted this "new world" with the gospel of Jesus Christ. We now have a new generation of Americans who have been raised in a godless culture for nearly sixty years. Like the generations during the time of the judges in Israel, we are witnessing a new generation that is evil in the sight of God.

Truth has become offensive to most Americans. They have "changed the truth of God into a lie" (Romans 1:25). Man's ideas about himself and the creation have replaced God's truth. Only a fool could think that His thoughts are greater than God's thoughts. How stupid and ridiculous! To these fools, God graciously sends out this invitation, "Seek ye the LORD while he may be found, call ye upon him while he is near: Let the wicked forsake his way, and the unrighteous man his thoughts: and let him return unto the LORD, and he will have mercy upon him; and to our God, for he will abundantly pardon. For my thoughts are not your thoughts, neither are your ways my ways, saith the LORD. For as the heavens are higher than the earth, so are my ways higher than your ways, and my thoughts than your thoughts" (Isaiah 55:6-9).

For example, we live at a time when America is being challenged to openly embrace and accept gay lifestyles. We are being asked to have an open mind and accept this is what some people want. Is this good? Are we really thinking about what is good for these people? Do we really want what is best for them? First, the Bible openly and repeatedly condemns homosexuality and any form of sex outside of the bonds of marriage between a man and a woman as sin and an offense against our holy God (Romans 1:24-32). Romans 1:27 indicates that sexually transmitted diseases are a form of God's judgment upon those who transgress His moral law. David Kupleian, writes: "…half of the gay and bisexual men will be HIV-positive by age 50."[2] Therefore, do we really care about the gay community? If we do, we must be brave enough to tell them the truth. They would call this hate speech. However, the Bible tells us that is really speaking the truth in love.

We live in a country where people have been warned about the dangerous and addictive effects of nicotine in cigarettes. Federal law requires that cigarette manufacturers must clearly label each package to state the dangers of their product. The biblical warning against homosexuality, along with medical research, clearly indicates that the gay lifestyle is dangerous to one's health. Moreover, it carries a deadly mental and spiritual impact upon individuals who practice it. Why does our culture accept the warning against nicotine, but reject the warning against such a promiscuous lifestyle? The answer is that people's standard of approval is based upon the subjective demands of the culture and not upon what the Bible declares is right or wrong. Man continues to adjust and change his moral compass based upon the thinking of the culture around him. This is wrong and it brings deadly consequences.

God's truth is based upon His character. His truth is perfect, infinite, and eternal, because He is perfect, infinite, and eternal. Since God does not change (Malachi 3:6); His truth does not change (Isaiah 40:8). God is also sovereign. He rules over all of His creation from His throne in heaven. He is the One who works "all things after the counsel of his own will" (Ephesians 1:11). Therefore, God's truth is absolute! Since God is the One who inhabits the eternal now, it is ridiculous to think in terms of God's absolute truth shifting or changing with the winds of time. We are finite creatures of time, space, and matter. However, God is not! God is eternal (Isaiah 57:15). God is omnipresent (everywhere present at the same moment throughout all of His creation- Psalm 139:1-12). God is not a physical being, but "is a spirit" (John 4:24). If this seems too difficult to grasp, welcome to the mind of our infinite God! "O the depth of the riches both of the wisdom and knowledge of God! How unsearchable are his judgments and his ways past finding out!" (Romans 11:33)

In Matthew 7, Jesus spoke to the religious crowd of His day who were walking in spiritual darkness. He gave them a solemn but truthful warning concerning their ultimate destiny. First, He warned them of their deceptive path. In Matthew 7:13-14, Jesus explained that the majority in a culture are not on the right path. He stated that there are only two paths – the right one and the wrong one. The wrong path is wide, accessible, and offers little resistance. Most people are traveling this path and the Bible warns that it is the path "that leadeth to destruction" (Matthew 7:13). The right path is through a narrow gate. This path is restrictive, unpopular, and it offers great resistance. Tragically, only a few people are traveling on this path "which leadeth unto life" (Matthew 7:14). Jesus clearly warned His audience they should not choose the most popular road in life. Why? Because the majority of people never walk with God!

Secondly, Jesus spoke about the deceptive prophets in His culture (Matthew 7:15-20). He clearly warned people to watch out for the false prophets who claimed to be messengers from God. He exhorted people to examine these prophets as they would a fruit tree. The real question

He posed is: Does the fruit match the root of its source? Therefore, we are to examine a preacher by comparing him to the only true root of truth – the Bible. If his teachings and lifestyle do not agree with the Bible, he is a false teacher. Our nation has far too many preachers whose message and lifestyle do not agree with the Bible. These deceptive teachers are leading their followers astray from God and His truth. These false prophets should be avoided at all costs.

Thirdly, Jesus spoke about <u>deceptive professions</u> of faith (Matthew 7:21-23). In this warning, Jesus spoke about the final judgment day when people will stand before the Lord, only to discover they have taken the <u>deceptive</u> path and listened to the <u>deceptive</u> prophets. <u>Deceptive</u> professions will not stand up in God's court because faith was not accompanied by works that were in agreement with "the will of my Father which is in heaven" (Matthew 7:21).

To illustrate His teaching about all of this, Jesus told them a parable about a wise man and a foolish man (Matthew 7:24-27). In this parable, there are two different men who made two different choices. The wise man built his house upon a rock. When the storm came, his house stood firm. On the other hand, the foolish man built his house upon the shifting sand. When the storm came, his house collapsed. What was Jesus teaching with this illustration? Both the wise man and the foolish man heard the words of Jesus (Matthew 7:24, 26). However, only the wise man obeyed the words of Jesus and applied them to his life. The foolish man simply ignored the words of Jesus. In this parable, the houses of these two men represent their lives. The wise man chose to build his life upon the solid rock of God's truth. When the storms of life came, and ultimately the judgment day, his life would stand the test, and he would be saved. However, the foolish man built his life upon the shifting sand. His life was founded upon the ways of the deceptive path and deceptive prophets in his culture. He chose to follow the subjective advice and lifestyle of his culture rather than the unchanging Word of God. The result for him was tragic. When he stands before God on his judgment day, his life will be lost. The foolish man always chooses the way of his culture rather than the Word of God. Clearly, Jesus was teaching that the foolish man always resists and suppresses the Word of God.

What about you? Are you building your life upon the Bible or the message of the American culture? Every day we are impacted by our culture. We watch television, surf the Internet, read books and magazines, read the billboards and signs on our roads, listen to the music of the world, respect or reject the opinions of others, etc. If this is all we think about and mentally embrace, then we will be like the foolish man that built his house upon the sand. Proverbs 23:7 states, "For as [a man thinks] in his heart so is he." Just like we physically become what we eat, even so we become spiritually what we think. There is only one way to be like the wise man – build your life upon the solid rock of God's truth. You must spend time in God's Word! Listen to the message of Romans 12:2, "And be not conformed to this world: but be ye transformed <u>by the renewing of your mind</u>, that ye may prove what is that good, and acceptable, and perfect, will of God." You must renew your mind by allowing God's Word to dictate to you what is right and wrong, what must be received and what must be discarded. If you do not do this, then your mind will become a garbage pit that stinks before God and will poison your soul for eternity! The Word of God is God's cleansing agent that will purify your mind and life. Are you in the Bible each day?

Fools reject the Word of God. They claim they are too busy. In their pride, they think they know what to do without God's instruction. Wise men recognize the foolishness of their heart and their desperate need to fill their minds with the Word of God. Are you a fool or a wise man?

3. He Satisfies Self

The third core sin of the fool is his overriding priority to satisfy self. The fool places his desires and perceived needs above all else. In his eyes, he is more important than God, his spouse, family, or friends. What he wants must come first. The fool will selfishly sacrifice everything for what he wants, no matter the consequences!

Proverbs 18:2 declares, "A fool hath no delight in understanding, but that his heart may discover itself." Proverbs 28:26 adds, "He that trusteth in his own heart is a fool..." At the heart of all of this is a priority of love for self.

Self-love is one of the core sins of the last days. Near the end of his ministry, the apostle Paul wrote, "This know also, that in the last days perilous times shall come. For men shall be lovers of their own selves ... lovers of pleasures more than lovers of God ... Ever learning, and never able to come to the knowledge of the truth" (2 Timothy 3:1-2, 4, 7).

Pleasure has a tendency to numb and desensitize the mind. Fools are always battling between what feels good and what is right. We all have a sin nature from the time of our birth (Proverbs 22:15) that is bound up in pleasing self. The fool thinks: "If it feels good, it must be right." Sinful pleasures have a way of deceiving and distracting us from their ultimate tragic consequences. Proverbs 14:12 warns us, "There is a way which seemeth right unto a man, but the end thereof are the ways of death."

Sinful pleasures are deceitful. (Hebrews 3:13) Our foolish mind often tempts us to enjoy "the pleasures of sin" forgetting they are only "for a season" (Hebrews 11:25). The message of the Bible from the beginning to the end is the same – "the wages of sin is death" (Romans 6:23). Sin is a cruel slave master. It has a powerful influence on us that is all too evident. Read what the apostle Paul had to say about this struggle against the slave master of sin in Romans 7:7-25.

Sin also carries an exceptionally heavy price tag. The fool does not think about this. In his foolish determination to please himself, he only thinks about immediate gratification. He does not think of the long-term consequences of his sin.

We live in a world that is pleasure mad! This includes sports, entertainment, music, movies, computer games, amusement parks, sex, food, travel, etc. People spend countless hours pleasing themselves without ever thinking of eternity and the consequences of their actions. This is the way it was in the days of Noah before the flood. These were the prevailing conditions in Sodom and Gomorrah before their divine judgment.

Listen to the testimony of King Solomon, who was the richest and wisest man of his time. After a life of enjoying whatever he wanted as the richest king of Israel, he testified to the emptiness of all of his wealth, pleasure, and popularity. Read Ecclesiastes 1-2. In Ecclesiastes 7:2-4, he gives us a valuable insight into the foolishness of the human heart. In this text, he testifies that it is more beneficial to go to a funeral than to attend a party. He declares that the sorrow at a funeral will make us think about eternity and the end of life, which is good. The good time at a party will numb your mind so that you will not think about the most important things in life. In verse 4, he says, "The heart of the wise is in the house of mourning; but the heart of fools is in the house of mirth."

Friend, what is the purpose of your life? Listen to Jesus' statement to His disciples in Matthew 16:24-26, "If any man will come after me, let him deny himself, and take up his cross, and follow me. For whosoever will save his life shall lose it; and whosoever will lose his life for my sake shall find it. For what is a man profited, if he shall gain the whole world, and lose his own soul? or what shall a man give in exchange for his soul?" If you follow Him, you will walk down the path that is least traveled in our culture. You will build your life upon the rock of Jesus and His Word. You will stop being a fool and will deny yourself and sacrificially make Jesus first in your life. If you choose to be the fool, you will have lost your soul and will spend eternity in hell. Don't be a fool!

CHAPTER 7

Living in a Culture of Deception

"Now the Spirit speaks expressly, that in the latter times some
shall depart from the faith, giving heed to seducing spirits,
and doctrine of [demons]; Speaking lies in hypocrisy;
having their conscience seared with a hot iron."
1 Timothy 4:1-2

WE ARE LIVING IN A WORLD FULL OF DECEPTION. Every time our phone rings, we have to be concerned that someone is trying to take advantage of us. When we stop at a stoplight, we see people standing on a corner holding up a sign trying to convince us to help them by giving them a donation. We have all heard that some of these people are professional liars who are trying to dupe us into supporting their sinful habits or entitlement mentality. We have all grown tired of politicians who parade lies before us to get our vote. We are even deceived at the grocery store. We purchase items only to discover when we go home that we purchased more air or box than the product we thought we were buying. We have all been given promises by our family and friends, only to be disappointed when they fail to keep their word – for the fourth time in two weeks.

We are surrounded by liars. These include those in the media, political arena at all levels, the educational and scientific fields of the academic world, the medical profession and pharmaceutical industry, and the religious charlatans that parade themselves as be messengers of God. In order to survive and thrive in this kind of world, we must rely upon the wisdom that comes from the Bible. The discernment between lies and truth comes only when we hold everyone and everything up to the standard of truth – God and His revelation, the Bible. God is a God of truth. He cannot lie! Therefore, only the Bible can give us wisdom to strip away deception so we can clearly see the truth!

Unfortunately, we live in a world where many people do not know truth. Sadly, they do not want to know the truth. They want to live and promote their lies to their own selfish advantage. Adolf Hitler, who was the leader of the Nazi Party and chancellor of Germany from 1933 to 1945, is a prime example of this fact. He searched for lies to advance His goals and promoted them with great passion. It is reported that he once said; "If you tell a big enough lie, and tell it frequently enough, it will be believed."

Many Americans' lives are currently being dominated by eight big lies of our time: 1.Our world is the present result of billions of years of evolution. 2. Islam is a religion of peace. 3. The unborn fetus is only the tissue of the mother. 4. Homosexuality is genetically hardwired in people. 5. Socialism is better than capitalism and democracy. 6. The U.S. constitution calls for a separation of church and state. 7. Man-made emissions are the major cause of dangerous levels of global climate change. 8. The Bible is not reliable. You can add many more to this list. However, these lies are constantly repeated by certain individuals to promote their self-centered agenda. All of these lies and liars stand in direct opposition to God and the Word of truth.

Most people in our culture are not being convicted of their sinful lifestyle of lying. They are like those mentioned in 1 Timothy 4:2 who have departed from the truth and are "speaking lies in hypocrisy; having their conscience seared with a hot iron." We have reached a point where people have actually bought into their own lies. Their lying has become so habitual that it has become the way they relate to others and do business in the market place. When they tell a lie, their conscience no longer strives with them to produce any guilt or shame. These people have no concern that they have offended God or defrauded someone else. Instead, many now seem to take great joy in deceiving others. It is almost like a game they love to play.

The message of the Bible is clear. God hates all lies and deception. "Lying lips are abomination to the LORD: but they that deal truly are his delight" (Proverbs 12:22). Proverbs 6:16-19, lists seven things that God hates. Two of these seven are the sin of lying. God says that "a lying tongue, and ... A false witness that speaks lies" are "an abomination unto Him" (Proverbs 6:16-17, 19). This solemn warning comes in Revelation 21:8, "All liars, shall have their part in the lake which burneth with fire and brimstone, which is the second death."

Why does God hate lying so much? Lying goes against God's character of flawless, eternal, and absolute truth. According to the Bible, God is the "LORD God of truth" (Psalm 31:5). When Jesus prayed for us in His high priestly prayer, He requested that we might know His Father is "the only true God" (John 17:3). These declarations are filled with meaning that is essential to our faith. It means the God of the Bible is the only genuine God. All other gods do not exist. They are fakes and frauds created by Satan and his demons. To say that God is true also affirms that God is all that He needs to be. As God, He is infinitely perfect and complete within Himself.

To say God is true, is to acknowledge that His words are reality – the way things really are. The Bible is God's statement about the reality of His character, words, and actions. While praying, Jesus said to His Father, "Thy word is truth" (John 17:17). This means the Bible is God's revelation about reality, which is grounded in the very nature of God. If God were to lie, it would be the end of the God of the Bible. Notice that Jesus said, *I am the way, the truth, and the life* (John 14:6). Truth and life are married to each other in the very nature of God. God and His Word are the flawless, eternal, universal standard. This truth is replicated throughout God's creation. The material universe is anchored in the unchanging nature of the God of truth. The creation is filled with complex order. The DNA structure of organisms, the atoms contained in all elements, and the millions of galaxies exist in a predictable order. Without this order the creation would cease to exist. Likewise, the moral standards recorded in the Bible are grounded in the very nature of the God of truth. God's declaration of good and evil is based upon His unchanging, eternal nature. Therefore, God's moral standards are for all people of all ages. God has designed His creation to self-destruct when these moral standards are violated. Obedience brings life, while disobedience brings death (Deuteronomy 30:15-19). This is a foundational truth that is being ignored or challenged in our day. When man attempts to alter or modify God's truth, he is making arrangements for his funeral and ultimate sentence on judgment day.

When people lie, they are putting themselves, and all others who hear them, in jeopardy of believing and following a deadly falsehood. We become what we think. "For as a he thinketh in his heart, so is he" (Proverbs 23:7). When we lie, we are opposing God and His truth. And, we are joining rank with the author of lies, the devil. Speaking of the devil, Jesus said, "He was a murderer from the beginning, and abode not in the truth, because there is no truth in him. When he speaketh a lie, he speaketh of his own: for he is a liar, and the father of it" (John 8:44). Those who endorse a lifestyle of deception and lies are promoting Satan's kingdom of darkness! They are promoters of immorality, wickedness, and death. When they lie, they are acting like their father, the devil.

According to the prophetic Word of God, the end of this age will be characterized as a time of dangerous spiritual deception! In Matthew 24:4-5, notice Jesus' first response to the disciples' question about the end of this age, "Take heed that no man deceive you. For many shall come in my name, saying, I am Christ: and shall deceive many." In verses 24-25, He continued: "For there shall arise false Christs, and false prophets, and shall show great signs and wonders; insomuch that, if it were possible, they shall deceive the very elect. Behold, I have told you before." According to Romans 1, when a culture has departed from God, it will consistently change "the truth of God into a lie" (verse 25). They invert reality. People are unknowingly attempting to alter the foundational nature of God, making Him a liar! This is at the heart of

Satan's efforts to defeat and dethrone God. He wants to make God a liar! In the beginning, when Satan tempted Eve, he basically called God a liar. (Genesis 3:1-5) The Lord has made thousands of prophetic statements about the presence of the nation of Israel on the stage of human history at the end of the age. Satan's goal is to destroy Israel so that God's Word will fail, making God a liar. Ultimately, when people lie, they are joining with the father of lies and unwittingly carrying out his hellish agenda.

Recently, Pope Francis began promoting the lie that the God of the Bible and Allah are one and the same. This is a lie! The stated character and goals of God and Allah in the Bible and Koran are incredibly different. They cannot be the same. The Pope also stated that the Bible and Koran are both divine holy books. Anyone who has seriously compared the doctrines of the Bible with the doctrines of the Koran knows that making these claims is absurd! These kinds of lies being disseminated by people of great influence illustrate the dangerous climate of deception in our times. These lies are promoting the eternal damnation of millions of souls.

Satan has a master plan of deception for the nations at the end of this age. In the final book of the Bible, Satan is known as the one who deceives "the whole world" (Revelation 12:9). Satan's deception will be so successful, that the Lord will lock him away so "that he should deceive the nations no more, till the thousand years should be fulfilled" (Revelation 20:3). Satan and his demons will be bound and cast into the bottomless pit for the entire millennial reign of Christ on earth. However, "when the thousand years are expired, Satan shall be loosed out of his prison, and shall go out to deceive the nations..." (Revelation 20:7-8).

Satan's greatest hour of deception will take place with his false messiah - the Antichrist. His appearance will be accompanied by "lying wonders" (2 Thessalonians 2:9). He and his false prophet will perform many miracles that will deceive the entire world (Revelation 13:11-15). As a result, an overwhelming majority of the world's population will believe the Antichrist is God. Consequently, they will worship him (Revelation 13:8).

Friends, we need to understand that this growing spirit of deception in our age is preparing our world for the greatest lie to be perpetrated upon mankind since the Garden of Eden. Our world is being conditioned to believe the lie of the Antichrist that will take place during the time of tribulation. In an amazing text, written by the apostle Paul almost 2,000 years ago, the Lord revealed to him in 2 Thessalonians 2:8-12, three reasons why the world will believe the damning lie that the Antichrist is God. While these verses speak about what will take place during the tribulation, we are now experiencing a culture of deception that is laying the foundation for this dangerous period of time. Let us examine this text and discover these three reasons that will promote this deadly deception:

Reason #1: They Love their Sin

Medical science has long told us that people are pleasure/pain individuals. We like to indulge in pleasure, while we seek to avoid pain at all cost. All pleasure is not sinful, but all sin is filled with pleasure for self! There is pleasure in sin "for a season" (Hebrews 11:25). Because of its temporary gratification, sin always has an appeal to our sinful nature that is bent on pleasing self rather than believing God and obeying Him. Sin is "the lust of the flesh, and the lust of the eyes, and the pride of life" (1 John 2:16). We live in a world that is suppressing "the truth in unrighteous" (Romans 1:18). When people suppress God's truth and cling to their sinful pleasures, they have reached a point of divine judgment (Romans 1:18-32). Their conscience is "darkened" (verse 21). As a result of a seared conscience, God will give over this generation "to uncleanness through the lusts of their own hearts, to dishonor their own bodies between themselves: Who changed the truth of God into a lie..." (verses 24-25). The end result is lesbianism (verse 26) and homosexuality (verse 27). These sins will also be accompanied by a physical penalty [sexually-transmitted diseases] (verse 27), due to their defiant rebellion against the moral truth of God. The proliferation of these lifestyles in the last days will create "perilous times" (2 Timothy 3:1). These dangerous days are directly linked to a self-centered lifestyle that leads people to be "lovers of pleasures more than lovers of God" (2 Timothy 3:4).

This kind of society that is bent on the pleasures of sin will set the stage for the lawless one, the Antichrist. In 2 Thessalonians 2, it is revealed that those who will be deceived and follow the Antichrist in the time of tribulation will do so because of "all deceivableness of unrighteousness in them" (verse 10). Verse 12 clearly indicts them as those who "had pleasure in unrighteousness." They will love and worship the Antichrist because he is promoting and living the sinful pleasures that appeal to them. This is what the godless governments of the world are already doing. Friends, it is clear that we have arrived at this hour! We live in a culture that is pleasure mad! We are suffering from the sin of "me-ism."

Reason #2- Their Lack of Love for the Truth

Another reason why the terminal generation of the tribulation will follow the deception of the Antichrist is because they will have no desire to believe or know the truth (2 Thessalonians 2:8-12). These people are described as those who "received not the love of the truth" (verse 10), and "believed not the truth" (verse 12). These people will ignore their conscience and God's revealed truth because they have made a willful decision that the pleasure of sin is more important than knowing God's truth and submitting to it. Eventually, they arrive at the place where they hate God and His truth (Romans 1:30). They will be filled with wickedness and they will militantly begin to defend their immoral lifestyle (Romans 1:29-31). Furthermore, they become "despisers of those that are good" (2 Timothy 3:3).

The knowledge of God's Word is the only lifeline for mankind living in a world of sin. If you do not know God's truth, then you do not know the standard of truth to which everything must be compared. We do not think like God. God says, "For my thoughts are not your thoughts, neither are your ways my ways, saith the LORD. For as the heavens are higher than the earth, so are my ways higher than your ways, and my thoughts than your thoughts" (Isaiah 55:8, 9). God's truth is infinite.

Our thoughts are not only limited, but greatly flawed by our sinful way of thinking. God says, "The heart is deceitful above all things, and desperately wicked" (Jeremiah 17:9). The Bible declares, "There is a way which seemeth right unto a man, but the end thereof are the ways of death" (Proverbs 14:12).

If we do not know the Bible, we are in big trouble. Being surrounded by liars and deceivers, we are vulnerable to follow the way of sinners, rather than the way of God. Read Psalm 1 to gain a grasp of this vital truth. The apostle Paul prayed that the early church believers would be filled with the knowledge of God. He said to them, "[I] do not cease to pray for you, and to desire that ye might be filled with the knowledge of his will in all wisdom and spiritual understanding; That ye might walk worthy of the Lord unto all pleasing, being fruitful in every good work, and increasing in the knowledge of God" (Colossians 1:9-10).

Alarmingly, we live at a time when the church is departing from the proclamation of the Word of truth. Pastors are twisting and minimizing the Scriptures, replacing them with their own philosophies, psychology, and entertaining stories (2 Timothy 4:1-4). All the while, their congregations are filled with people who enjoy a message that does not bring conviction and repentance. In essence, pastors and churches are not carrying out their mission of reconciling lost people to a holy God! We live in a day when people in churches that do hear the truth, become offended and start a crusade to get rid of the pastor. They may leave the church where truth is being proclaimed and start shopping for a church that will tell them what they want to hear.

The biblical illiteracy of our age is frightening! Professing believers do not know the Bible any better than people who do not attend church. Concerning this, Dr. Albert Mohler, a well-known theologian and president of Southern Baptist Theological Seminary, states, "Fewer than half of all adults can name the four gospels. Many Christians cannot identify more than two or three of the disciples. According to data from the Barna Research Group, 60 percent of Americans can't name even five of the Ten Commandments." [1] This crisis in biblical illiteracy has prepared our world for the deception of the Antichrist.

Reason #3- They Are Lost in Spiritual Darkness

The passage under consideration, 2 Thessalonians 2:8-12, is not speaking about those who are lost and reject the truth during the church age before the Rapture. Notice that verses 8-10 are one sentence. This is clearly a text that is speaking about developments connected to the Antichrist during the time of the tribulation. Consequently, this text should not be used to teach that those who reject the gospel before the Rapture cannot be saved during the tribulation. It is best to compare this passage with Revelation 13-14. In both passages, people will have believed the lie of the Antichrist and worship him. In each passage the Antichrist is a promoter of lying wonders and miracles. In both texts, those who accept the lie are eternally damned and they cannot be saved. Revelation 14:9-11 makes it clear that anyone who will receive the mark of the Antichrist, the number of his name – 666, is eternally damned and cannot be saved.

In 2 Thessalonians 2, those who are "damned" (verse 12) are those who "perish; because they received not the love of the truth, that they might be saved" (verse 10). This tribulation generation will have been so deceived they will willfully and defiantly reject the truth they have heard from the 144,000 Jewish evangelists (Revelation 7:1-8) and the flying angel (Revelation 14:6-7). These messengers from God will have given the gospel to all the nations in all languages before the Antichrist introduces himself to the world as god and forces his 666 number upon all of them. At some point during their defiant rebellion, the Lord will justifiably "send them strong delusion, that they should believe [the] lie: That they all might be damned who believed not the truth, but had pleasure in unrighteousness" (2 Thessalonians 2:11-12).

Friends, it is not just a coincidence that we are witnessing global anarchy over the demands of those who are passionately living for pleasure in their sin. Those who are planning a new world order are helping to promote this era of lawlessness. They are fueling radical Islam and those bent on sexual freedom to foment this rebellion against law and order. This is the force that is behind the orchestrated revolt against the constitutional government of the United States. Those who are playing along with the socialists in this growing opposition are attempting to destroy America in order to create a socialist new world order that will be politically married to Islam. When this happens, it will, in effect, roll out the red carpet for the Antichrist and his kingdom of darkness.

As true believers in Jesus Christ, we need to be driven to the Word of God. We are children of the light, not of the darkness. It is time for the church to wake up and stand up for the truth. We need to be salt and light in this world (Matthew 5:13-16). We will be hated and rejected, but we must stand for the truth. The words in Ephesians 5:8-14 seem to be so appropriate for this time. We must redeem "the time, because the days are evil" (Ephesians 5:16).

CHAPTER 8

Violence and the End of a Culture

"And God said unto Noah, The end of all flesh is
come before me; for the earth is filled
with violence through them; and, behold, I
will destroy them with the earth."
Genesis 6:13

HAVE YOU EVER WONDERED WHAT GOD SEES AND hears as He looks down upon the earth each day? The Bible tells us that God is everywhere present in His creation. He sees, hears and knows everything that is happening each moment, both in heaven and on earth. He knows the thoughts of every creature, both mankind and angels (Jeremiah 17:10). God never learns. He is never surprised. He knows every person on the planet by name. He knows everything about them.

While speaking about the value of a person, Jesus reminded His disciples that in His divine providence, God governs all and He is aware of the smallest details. Jesus said not one sparrow can fall to the ground without the Father's knowledge. Furthermore, God has every hair on the head of every person numbered (Matthew 10:29-30). The psalmist said, "Such knowledge is too wonderful for me; it is high, I cannot attain unto it" (Psalm 139:6). What a God! He is truly beyond our human comprehension!

Nothing can be hidden from God's eyes. Psalm 33:13-14 says, "The LORD looketh from heaven; he beholdeth all the sons of men. From the place of his habitation he looketh upon all the inhabitants of the earth." In Psalm 14:2, the Bible declares, "The LORD looked down from heaven upon the children of men to see if there were any that did understand, and seek God." In the context of this psalm, the conclusion to God's search is given. "The fool hath said in his heart, There is no God. They are corrupt, they have done abominable works, there is none that doeth good. ... They are all gone aside, they are altogether become filthy: there is none that doeth good, no, not one" (Psalm 14:1 and 3).

In the beginning, God created everything for His glory and for His praise. How God must be grieved every day as He gazes down upon 7.6 billion people that inhabit this planet. We can only wonder what captures God's holy attention as he gazes down at His creation. Nothing escapes His knowledge, not even the smallest detail. In Genesis 6, God looked out over the global population in Noah's time. "And God saw that the wickedness of man was great in the earth, and that every imagination of the thoughts of his heart was only evil continually" (verse 5). The magnitude of man's wickedness "grieved [God] at his heart" (verse 6). It was this grief that caused the holy Lord of the Bible to declare that He was going to send a global flood to destroy everyone who was not on the ark.

When you read God's indictment in Genesis 6, it is abundantly clear there were two sins that God's eyes were riveted upon each day as He gazed upon humanity. He was grieved because of their sexual corruption and brutal violence (Genesis 6:11-13). Earlier in Genesis 6, God declared, "My spirit shall not always strive with man" (Genesis 6:3). Many Bible scholars agree this is a reference to the work of the Holy Spirit in the conscience of man. God was declaring that man can come to a point when His Spirit ceases striving in the conscience of man.

The Bible teaches that a person can gradually defile his conscience to the point that it is ultimately silenced or "seared" (1Timothy 4:2).

When this happens to enough people, the culture collectively reaches the spiritual point of no return and it is slated for divine judgment. A study of the context of Genesis 6, and the greater context of all of God's revelation, indicates there are two things that defile the conscience of man – sexual immorality and violence.

It has come to my attention that most believers, and the church as a whole, do not understand the impact of violence on the conscience. Some may grasp the impact of sexually immorality upon the conscience. However, the church has been almost completely silent in addressing the dangers of violence. It is the purpose of this chapter to expose and address the biblical view of violence and its impact upon our global culture in light of the Word of God.

Most people are so engrossed in their own little world they have not stopped to assess the fact we are living at a time of incredible global violence. In America and around the world, we are experiencing a tsunami of violence. The senseless violence we have seen in Chicago illustrates this. In 2015, there were 485 homicides in Chicago. A year later, the number of victims skyrocketed to 764. That was 58 percent more homicides and 43 percent more nonfatal shootings in 2016.

Since September 11, 2001, leading historians and policymakers around the world have referred to our times as "the age of terror." At home and abroad, we are being exposed to the rising threat of Islamic terrorism. The violent images of atrocities committed by ISIS, Boko Haram, and a host of other extremist terrorist organizations have been broadcast across the planet by our media. The carnage of war and the loss of life due to advanced weaponry of war are alarming. The growing displacement of refugees fleeing from war-torn Middle Eastern countries is creating a logistical nightmare – and it is being accompanied by the spread of global Islamic terrorism among the Western nations.

In addition, the dramatic increase we are experiencing in domestic violence is frightening. We have violence in our schools, homes, churches, synagogues, airports, and many other public places. We talk about road rage, bullying, violence against women and children, and the savage brutality against the unborn. Violence is marketed as entertainment in our culture. Many Americans come home from work or school to watch hours of programming that features graphic violence. Bloody violence and murder permeate the entertainment industry. Violence is reaching our children through cartoons, musical lyrics, videos, and television programming. This means that our next generation is being systematically programmed to accept violence as a way of life. As a result, violence will continue to fester and reach epic proportions. Lawlessness will rule our world!

Statistical data show that there are more than 1.5 million people incarcerated in state and federal prison systems in America. The United States has more people per capita incarcerated in its prison systems than any nation in the world. And, the number and costs of these incarcerations keeps increasing at an alarming rate. In 1985, the collective state prison systems cost $6.7 billion. Now they cost more than $60 billion.

Before we turn to the Bible to examine what it has to say about violence, please read what a conservative secular group, *The Media Education Foundation*, has to say about violence in America.

- "Research indicates that media violence has not just increased in quantity; it has also become more graphic, sexual, and sadistic."
- "By the time the average child is 18 years old, they will have witnessed 200,000 acts of violence and 16,000 murders."
- "Media violence is especially damaging to young children (under 8) because they cannot easily tell the difference between real life and fantasy."
- "Most of the top-selling video games (8 percent) contained violent content, almost half of which was of a serious nature."
- "The level of violence during Saturday morning cartoons is higher than the level of violence during prime time. There are three to five violent acts per hour on prime time, versus 20 to 25 acts per hour on Saturday morning."
- "Nearly 75 percent of violent scenes on television feature no immediate punishment for or condemnation of violence." [1]

Let us now examine four Biblical considerations about violence:

1. The Biblical Definition of Violence

One of the most common Hebrew words translated "violence" in the Old Testament is "hamas." [Note that this is the same name chosen by the terrorist group that controls the Palestinian people in Gaza Strip that border Egypt and Israel. The world does not understand the situation in Gaza but Israel does. These people have chosen the name "violence" as a true expression of who they are. They are in the face of Israelis, threatening to murder them and destroy the nation of Israel.] The word "hamas" speaks of bringing great harm to people physically and mentally. It points to an act that is destructive, hateful, lawless, disrespectful, wicked, wild, ruthless, or brutal. It is usually accompanied by loud expressions of hatred. Violence is not only an act but is also verbalized as a demonstration of hatred. Proverbs 10:6 says, "… but violence covers the mouth of the wicked."

Violence is an action, gesture, or expression due to a lack of moral restraint. Its aim is to destroy, shame, maim, kill, or terrorize its victim. Violence is an expression of defiance and disrespect for the very basic code of behavior that the Spirit of God desires to instill in the conscience of mankind. Violence and its ultimate expression –murder – are the exact opposites of the character and nature of God (1 John 3:11-16). Jesus said that Satan "was a murderer from the beginning" (John 8:44). When people are moved by hatred to commit acts of violence, they are acting like the devil, not God.

Violence and murder draw immediate attention from God. God said to Cain after he slew his brother, Abel, "… the voice of thy brother's blood crieth unto me from the ground" (Genesis 4:10). This was not an isolated reaction from God. When God established human government, He instituted capital punishment as the cornerstone of governmental law to protect those who had been created in His image. He said, "Whoso shedeth man's blood, by man shall his blood be shed: for in the image of God made he man" (Genesis 9:6). Read Numbers 35:29-34. God told Israel that the shed blood of a person through murder defiles the land

and demands divine judgment. The only way to cleanse the land was to kill the murderer.

The 10 Commandments are aimed at a reverence for God and respect for human beings. They are the code of conduct that maintains the very foundation of life in any society. Thus, violence is the result of a total departure from this law and its author – God! In essence, a violent culture is in a mode of self-destruction! "If the foundations be destroyed, what can the righteous do?" (Psalm 11:3)

2. The Cultural Impact of Violence

When expressions of violence are allowed to permeate a culture, they will create a society that is void of a godly conscience. This leads to increasing levels of wickedness, lawlessness, sensuality, and brutality. This is clearly demonstrated in two New Testament passages – Romans 1:18-32 and 2 Timothy 3:1-9. Notice these passages speak of brutality, murder, hatred, and disrespect for God and man. Part of the work of the Spirit of God in the conscience of man is to create an atmosphere of peace, respect, and submission to the rule of law that God intended to be enforced by human government. It is God's design that his work in man's conscience and the rule of law created and maintained by human government are to complement one another (Romans 13:5). This is one of the reasons why Paul instructed Timothy to pray for those who "are in authority; that we may lead a quiet and peaceable life in all godliness and honesty. For this is good and acceptable in the sight of God our Savior; who will have all men to be saved, and to come unto the knowledge of the truth" (1 Timothy 2:2-4).

It should be understood that the ability to effectively share the gospel in a culture is directly connected to the levels of respect for mankind that are promoted within that society. When violence is allowed to permeate a culture, it not only leads to dangerous times, but also the gospel is hindered. The effectual working of the Holy Spirit through the gospel is hampered because of the explosion of violence in a society where the collective conscience of people has been seared. The conscience is where the Holy Spirit strives with lost men to convict them of their sin and bring them to Christ. When people in a culture reach a spiritual point of no return, divine judgment takes place and their consciences are darkened (Romans 1:21). In essence, God gives them up (Romans 1:24-27)! These same rebels no longer want "to retain God in their knowledge" (Romans 1:28). They become "haters of God" (Romans 1:30).

Jesus' parable of the sower and the seed in Matthew 13:1-23, gives us a perfect illustration of this. In this parable, as Jesus explained to His disciples, the person sowing the seed is the evangelizer and the seed is the gospel. The types of the soil in the parable are conditions of the human heart [conscience]. The seed that falls on the hard pathway does not penetrate into the soil for germination to take place. Consequently, the birds come and snatch up the seed. Later, Jesus explained what happened to the seed that was sown in a hardened heart, "Then cometh the wicked one, and catcheth away that which was sown in his heart" (verse 19). Jesus explained that the birds that took away the seed (the gospel) were demons. The apostle Paul clearly elaborated upon the truth illustrated in this parable. In 1 Timothy 4:1-2, he described how some people deny the teaching of the Bible, while at the same time cling to deceptive teachings promoted by demons. The lives of these people are marked by hypocrisy and a seared conscience.

Therefore, one of the results of a culture where violence has become prevalent is an open and defiant hatred for the God of the Bible and the visible suppression of His truth revealed in Scripture. The growth of Islam among the nations is a clear sign that the global culture has reached the point of no return. Islam promotes violence against innocent human beings, especially the followers of Christ and the Jewish people. Islamic militants take sheer delight in committing graphic acts of brutality and terrorism against innocent people [including children and babies], proving they do not believe that man was created in the image of Almighty God. Furthermore, Islam vehemently rejects the gospel of Jesus Christ.

It is shocking to watch the growing number of Americans and popular Christian leaders who embrace Islam. At the same time, the church and the teachings of the Bible are being openly assailed and criticized. Why? Islam does not provide conviction against the unrighteous lifestyles within the godless American culture. On the other hand, the message of the Bible does bring condemnation and conviction. Jesus told us that this is why the world hated Him and why it will hate us. Read John 15:18-16:1. In America, hatred for Christians is escalating, and the moral values of the Bible are being openly and violently rejected like never before.

3. The Divine Judgment Due to the Permeation of Violence in a Culture

A study of the Bible and human history will demonstrate that when every culture came to its end, it was always filled with violence. When you examine all of the great superpowers of the past, such as the Roman Empire, it is evident that when each one came to its end, it was filled with violence.

When individuals in a culture reach the spiritual point of no return, it seems to speed up the rate of violence, hastening their divine judgment. As Proverbs 29:16 states, "When the wicked are multiplied, transgression increaseth." Sinners seem to embolden one another in their defiant rebellion against God and man. In other words, the increase in the magnitude and frequency of violence has a snowballing effect upon a culture. As the snowball rolls down the hill, it gets bigger and gains momentum. It is apparent that our global culture is experiencing this now.

While commenting on the violence during the days of Noah in Genesis 6:11, Matthew Henry wrote: "There was no order nor regular government; no man was safe in the possession of that which he had … there was nothing but murders, rapes, and [stealing]. … Take away conscience and the fear of God, and men become beasts and devils to one another, like fishes of the sea, where the greater devour the less. Sin fills the earth with violence, and so turns the world into a wilderness, into a cock-pit."

Biblical and secular history demonstrates that violent cultures destroy themselves. Then, God sends another nation to conquer them, completing the cycle of His divine judgment. In essence, this divine judgment is an act of mercy on the part of God. If these violent cultures were allowed to continue unrestrained, they would become a threat to the entire global population, just like in the days of Noah. God stops brutal regimes. He visits "the iniquity of the fathers upon the children unto the third and fourth generation of them that hate [Him]" (Exodus 20:5). We can be thankful that God in His infinite wisdom and mercy limits wickedness. God does have a toleration point! He demonstrated that when He destroyed Sodom and Gomorrah and when He caused Israel to drive the Canaanites out of the land. Many generations later, God sent in the Assyrians and Babylonians to bring divine judgment upon His own people because of their violence and wickedness (Ezekiel 7:23-24). Then, in turn, He caused Assyria and Babylon to fall because of their violence and wickedness. This has been the common course of human history since the fall of man in the Garden of Eden. According to the Bible, when the end comes, it will be a time of violence that will surpass all levels of brutality in the history of the planet (Daniel 12:1; Matthew 24:21, 22).

4. Concluding Biblical Admonitions Concerning Violence

Violence has terrorized mankind throughout human history. From the murder of Abel to the crushing forces of the Antichrist at Armageddon, violence has grieved the heart of God.

God hates violence! Jesus will rule the world from Jerusalem for 1,000 years. His government will not tolerate violence. In Isaiah 60:18 God gave the following promise to His people, "Violence shall no more be heard in thy land." Among the Gentile nations, war and conflict will not be permitted. Finally, the world will have a righteous King who will also be the judge of all nations. "And he shall judge among the nations, and shall rebuke many people: and they shall beat their swords into plowshares, and their spears into pruning hooks; nation shall not lift up sword against nation, neither shall they learn war any more" (Isaiah 2:4).

The Lord exhorts His people to live in peace with everyone.

"Recompense to no man evil for evil. Provide things honest in the sight of all men. If it be possible, as much as lieth in you, live peaceably with all men. Dearly beloved, avenge not yourselves, but rather give place unto wrath: for it is written, Vengeance is mine; I will repay, saith the Lord" (Romans 12:17-19).

Violence is a serious matter to God and it stresses the utmost importance of guarding your conscience. We must protect our consciences by refraining from viewing or listening to violent expressions of any kind. We must not permit violence to enter our homes or minds with any level of acceptance or pleasure!

We must guard what enters our minds and consciences through the gates of our eyes, ears, and mouth. Proverbs 4:23 warns us, "Keep thy heart [conscience] with all diligence; for out of it are the issues of life." This is especially critical for small children who are in their foundational years when their conscience is impressionable.

When God looks down upon all mankind each day and sees all the violence and wickedness, His heart is broken. The wickedness of mankind in Noah's day grieved God's heart. This also was God's reaction to the wickedness of Sodom and Gomorrah. In Genesis 18:20 God exclaimed, "the cry of Sodom and Gomorrah is great, and … their sin is very grievous." I am often reminded of the tears of Jesus when He wept over Jerusalem and He said, "O Jerusalem, Jerusalem, thou that killest the prophets, and stoneth them which are sent unto thee, how often would I have gathered thy children together even as a hen gathereth her chickens under her wings, and ye would not" (Matthew 23:37)! Oh what love! The human mind cannot comprehend the infinite love of God.

God's love for us was so great that He permitted His Son to suffer for us on the cruel cross of Calvary. Although Jesus "had done no violence" (Isaiah 53:9), "yet it pleased the LORD to bruise him" (Isaiah 53:10). Jesus was "stricken, smitten of God, and afflicted" (Isaiah 53:4). Oh how the Father must love us!

Jesus suffered abuse and violence of a horrific death on a cross to pay for the penalty of all of our sins. He "became obedient unto death, even the death of the cross. Wherefore, God also hath highly exalted him, and given him a name which is above every name: That at the name of Jesus every knee should bow, of things in heaven, and things in earth, and things under the earth; And that every tongue should confess that Jesus Christ is Lord, to the glory of God the Father" (Philippians 2:8-11).

CHAPTER 9

Pornography – The Conscience Killer

"Dearly beloved, I [urge] you as strangers and pilgrims [on this earth], abstain from fleshly lusts, which war against the soul."
1 Peter 2:11

A S OUR DESIGNER AND CREATOR, GOD KNOWS OUR weakness and strengths. God has given us common sense to alert us to the many dangers we must avoid to escape serious injury or death. For example, we know we cannot jump off of a high building. Our bodies are not made for that kind of impact. We cannot live in an environment without oxygen for more than a few minutes. We cannot sustain long periods in extremely hot or cold temperatures. Likewise, our minds are not made to look upon nudity without mental and spiritual consequences. A constant steady diet of pornography can cause great damage to our conscience, ultimately leading to its destruction.

Pornography is a conscience killer. All porn is designed to cause lust that leads to immoral thoughts about another person. God has not designed the body to be aroused by viewing the nudity of a person who is not our spouse. Sexual arousal was designed by God to create a passionate and loving hunger to share the gift of sex with our spouse. It is called foreplay. When porn is used to evoke sexual arousal, it creates an unnatural and sinful set of circumstances. Pornographic images mentally force an individual into a passionate level of lust and desire that is ultimately fed outside of the God-ordained context of marriage. In addition, the constant diet of viewing porn will weaken the conscience. This occurs because the individual becomes more focused upon their sexual fantasy, while not thinking about the consequences. All too often, an innocent person becomes the object of their sexual fantasy, ultimately leading to forms of sexual immorality, including marriage infidelity, sex for hire, and rape.

In biblical times, nakedness was considered shameful and a sinful. In ancient times, the reference to nakedness was not complete nudity, but in some cases, it referred to a person wearing what we would call underwear. The Bible condemns the shameful practice of wearing scanty clothing in public. In our culture this is called "soft porn." The Bible condemns soft porn as well has hard-core porn. Partial nudity causes lust in the same ways that hard-core porn does. Television commercials clothing advertisements are filled with soft-porn!

God has given us multiple warnings about looking upon people's nakedness. It is a sin to uncover the nakedness of another person (Leviticus 18:6-18). Ham, the youngest son of Noah, was cursed because he looked upon his father's nakedness in his tent (Genesis 9:20-24). God warned Israel that during the construction of the altar at the tabernacle, they were not to have a ramp or stairs that the priest would climb to make sacrifice. This warning was given so as to not allow the priest (wearing a long, flowing robe) to expose himself to others around the altar. In Exodus 20:26, God said, "Neither shalt thou go up by steps unto mine altar, that thy nakedness be not discovered thereon." In Habakkuk 2:15 God warned, "Woe unto him that giveth his neighbor drink, that putteth thy bottle to him, and maketh him drunken also, that thou mayest look on their nakedness!"

Like previous ancient cultures that made pornography and sensual experiences a part of their normal routine, our American culture is immersed in sensuality. We routinely see seductively-dressed people throughout our communities. I must tell you that I have been amazed at how some women and girls dress when they attend church. Where are the godly parents or husband? Not too long ago, I saw an attractive young woman walk down the aisle of a large church. She had on a very seductive dress that revealed far too much. As she walked to her seat, I noticed the eyes of dozens of men as they turned their heads, following her every step. Those men, old and young, were in a state of lust. How do I know? They watched far too long! No man can do that without lusting. Many times I have said: "Today, some women come to church dressed like prostitutes dressed only 60 years ago."

If a man wants to keep his eyes from wandering and his heart from lusting, he must really set his mind to be godly and cry out to the Lord for help. Temptation is all around us.

Statistical data indicates the majority of men in our culture are addicted to pornography. The availability of porn on the Internet has made it easy to access for anyone who has a computer or electronic device. It is literally only a click away! As a result of this epidemic, by 2017 five states had declared pornography as a public health crisis. Statistics indicate that in America alone, half of the teenagers and nearly three-quarters of young adults view pornography on a monthly basis.

With this in mind, let us turn to the Bible to see what it says about porn.

1. Sexual lust is a burning desire (mental thought) that is a violation of God's moral law. Porn feeds such lust. It is like pouring gas on the fire of lust. It will create a burning passion that will get out of control, destroying everyone in its path.

The Bible warns us that the <u>physical act</u> of sexual sin is a direct result of the <u>mental thought</u> of lusting. The Bible says, "But every man is tempted, when he is draw away of his own lust, and enticed. Then when <u>lust</u> has conceived, it brings forth <u>sin</u>: and sin, when it is finished, brings forth <u>death</u>" (James 1:14-15). Notice the progression. First, the person mentally lusts. That is naturally followed by the physical act of sin. And when sin has arrived it always carries the penalty of death (separation from a holy God)! Viewing porn may seem harmless and it may bring momentary pleasure, but it carries a very heavy price tag.

Jesus connected the physical act of sexual sin with mental lusting when He said, "Ye have heard that is was said by them of old, Thou shalt not commit adultery: But I say unto you, That whosoever looketh on a woman to lust after her hath committed adultery with her already in his heart" (Matthew 5:27-28). Lusting is a sin, and the first step that leads to sexual immorality. Therefore, the first step toward having victory over porn is controlling sexual lust. The only way to do that is to not look! It is that constant looking that will get you in trouble. Look away. Cause your mind to refocus upon something more wholesome. The Bible says in Colossians 3:2, "Set your affection on things above, not on things on the earth." Turning from lust is about controlling the eyes and the mind to not be fixed upon someone who is causing you to potentially look too long with sinful pleasure in mind. Don't pamper yourself or lie to yourself and think you can control your mind and not have lustful thoughts. The goal is to have a conscience that will immediately fill your mind with fear of the consequences of lusting. It does not matter how young or old you are. Old men struggle with lust just like young men. I like to compare this with the danger of playing with a deadly snake. I just want to get away from the situation. I want a moment of fearful reverence for God, not a moment of sinful pleasure.

God has created us as sexual creatures. The Bible consistently teaches that sex within the marriage of a man and woman is precious in His sight (Hebrews 13:4). God not only created us to have sex for reproduction purposes, but to enjoy it as a gratifying pleasure within marriage. Read Proverbs 5:15-19. Notice that God said He wants the husband to be ravished with the intimate, physical, sexual love of his wife. God wants a man and wife to bring sexual pleasure to each other.

When a man and his wife share their physical, intimate sexual gifts with each other, they are responding in a way that God has made them. The wife responds to the warm and affectionate touch of her husband. That is why in 1 Corinthians 7:1-2, the Bible warns a man to not touch (fondly embrace) a woman who is not his wife. However, men have been made by God to be sexually stimulated by what they see. Remember the story of King David? When he saw a beautiful woman (Bathsheba) bathing, he lusted and that lust led to adultery. That act of adultery brought circumstances that created a lot of problems in David's life (2 Samuel 11-12). In the oldest book of the Bible, Job said, "I made a covenant with mine eyes: why should I think upon a maid?" (Job 31:1)

When a man looks at porn, he is creating a fire of lust in his mind. God has made the male mind and body to respond to the sensual display of a woman's body. This is normal, but God warned us in the Bible that this kind of burning desire is to be controlled and contained only for the purposes of sexual intimacy in marriage. While speaking about a young man lusting after a woman who is not his wife, the Lord has commanded, "Lust not after her beauty in your heart; neither let her [capture] you with her eyelids. ... Can a man take fire in his bosom, and his clothes not be burned? Can one go upon hot coals, and his feet not be burned? So he that goeth in to his neighbor's wife: whosoever toucheth her shall not be innocent" (Proverbs 6:25, 27-29). Our <u>physical</u> bodies have not been created to touch fire. In a similar fashion, we have not been made to <u>mentally</u> lust after the sensual display of a woman's body without sinful consequences. <u>No man can look intently at porn or gaze upon a provocatively-dressed woman and not lust!</u> It is the natural and sinful thing that will always happen. When a person is seeking to have a perfect heart before God, he "will set no wicked thing before [his] eyes" (Psalm 101:3).

When a person becomes addicted to porn, it will change his life. It will change who he is and what he thinks about other people. Our character is developed by the thoughts we repeatedly ponder in our mind. The Bible says, "For as [a man] thinks in his heart, so is he" (Proverbs 23:7). Our thoughts are like seeds that are planted. The Bible says that whatever we plant, we will reap. "Be not deceived: God is not mocked: for whatever a man soweth, that shall he also reap. For he that soweth to his flesh [sinful nature] shall of the flesh reap corruption; but he that soweth to the Spirit shall of the Spirit reap life everlasting" (Galatians 6:7-8).

When men constantly give their eyes and mind to pornography, they find it increasingly difficult to look at other women without lustful thoughts. They do not look at women and respect them nor honor them as another person created in the image of God. They are not thinking about the value of their soul or life. They are not thinking about the fact they are someone's child, parent, or spouse. They are only thinking about their sensual, selfish desires that are focused only upon personal instant gratification. This is a sin. It is wrong. It is shameful. When people constantly do this, and have no shame, they have effectively silenced their conscience.

2. All willful sin, including porn, will silence our God-given conscience.

Few people understand how deliberate sinful thoughts or actions impact our God-given conscience. Only man has been created in the image of God (Genesis 1:26-27). Like God, mankind is a moral person with a will. We make choices every day. God has created our inner being with a spiritual warning system called the conscience. The Holy Spirit is the One who works in us through our conscience. When we have sinful thoughts or commit sinful deeds, the Holy Spirit produces fear and shame within our inner being to condemn us. This is intended to warn us to stay away from those things that will harm or kill us. The Spirit of God will lead us to repentance - to turn away from sin and to God. God really does care about us and He wants us to know Him in an intimate way. God wants us to live for Him, and please Him. When we have good thoughts that are pleasing to God, our conscience does not accuse us. We are free to enjoy what God says is good.

God expects us to obey Him immediately. When His Spirit speaks to us through our conscience, He desires for us to obey Him at that moment. When we say "no" or "wait" to God, we will harden our heart [conscience]. In Hebrews 3:13, this is called "the deceitfulness of sin." Sin is deeply deceptive. People do not realize how deadly sin is – it is far more than just a game. Some Christians have a tendency to think they can sin, then pray and ask for forgiveness. Under this realm of thought, the slate is wiped clean as if they had never sinned. It is true that when we confess our sins, God does forgive us of all of our sins (1 John 1:9). However, that does not erase the impact that that sin has on your conscience. You may ask God to forgive you for looking at porn, but that will not instantly renew your conscience.

Our conscience is a like a muscle. It can be made stronger or it can become weaker. It is very important to have a strong conscience because we need God's help to say away from the deadly consequences of sin.

We can strengthen our conscience by feeding it the Word of God. The godly man in Psalm 119 said, "Thy word have I hid in my heart [conscience], that I might not sin against God" (verse 11). The Bible is the "truth." God's Word is the eternal, absolute truth. When we meditate upon the Bible and commit it to memory, we are planting God's standard in our conscience. This will enable the Holy Spirit to use this powerful standard to guide us and empower us when the temptation comes to fall into the trap of sin. It is a well known fact that the holy Word of God will have a purifying effect upon people. It will change their heart and equip them to live righteously for God. It changes our desires, motives, and goals in life.

According to the Bible, when the Holy Spirit warns us through our conscience about sin, and we ignore His warning, it will gradually weaken our conscience. When we do not listen to the Holy Spirit's warning it gets easier and easier to sin because our conscience is getting weaker. In fact, this condition of rebellion can reach a spiritual point of no return. This happens when the conscience is completely silenced by that person's consistent and flagrant rebellion against God's moral laws. Therefore, the Holy Spirit cannot work in them to bring repentance. Consequently, God gives up on them and the Holy Spirit permanently leaves them. So, they are left to follow their rebellious path to eternal damnation. Read Romans 1:18-32 and 1 Timothy 4:1-2.

Not only are we to strengthen our conscience, but we are to guard it from all evil. Like a computer, we are always programming our conscience with good or evil. EVERYTHING we see, hear and experience is registered in our brain and can be recalled at times. Therefore, it is important to refrain from all evil that will weaken our conscience. Read Proverbs 4:23-27. This passage reminds us that we must guard our heart [conscience] "for out of it are the issues of LIFE" (Proverbs 4:23). The Bible tells us to stay away from evil situations and evil people.

When people make porn a part of their lifestyle, they are destroying their inner man. (Please meditate on that statement! Let it sink deep into your mind and spirit.) Proverbs 6:32 says, "But whoso committeth adultery [mentally or physically] lacks understanding: he that doeth this destroyeth his own soul." Porn is a very cruel sin master. It will enslave you. It will trap you and destroy everything precious that God wants you to have and enjoy. Listen to Proverbs 5:20-23. "And why will you, my son, be ravished with a strange woman; and embrace the bosom of a stranger? For the ways of a man are before the eyes of the LORD, and he ponders all his goings. His own iniquities shall take the wicked himself, and he shall be held [entrapped] with the cords of his sin. He shall die without instruction; and in the greatness of his folly he shall go astray."

3. We must not ignore the demonic connection to porn and immorality.

Both history and the Bible testify to the demonic connection to immorality and pornography. During my many travels to the cradle of civilization in the Middle East, I have observed the archeological remains of ancient civilizations. It is abundantly clear that they were deeply immersed in many forms of sexual immorality. Many of their statues and reliefs are nothing more than pornography in stone! I will never forget my visit to ancient Ephesus several years ago. Our tour group walked down the main street of this city toward the remains of the ancient library of the first century. Along the street were replicas of the statues that were there when the apostle Paul founded a church in that city in the first century. These statues and others in the local museums depicted gross immoral activities of various kinds, both heterosexual and homosexual. It is clear that the Greek culture of Paul's day was deeply immersed in an avalanche of sexual perversions. A study of history will show that when these ancient cultures collapsed from within, it was in part because of immoral decay. This observation is confirmed by the

Bible. According to Genesis 6, it was this kind of lewdness that led to the divine destruction of Noah's civilization. Demons have always played a role in their immoral demise of a civilization.

Satan and his demons are biblically described as murderers (John 8:44) and destroyers (Revelation 9:11). One of the ways demons destroy people is by luring them to disobey or ignore God's moral laws. Many times in the gospels, demons are called "unclean spirits." Read the account of Jesus casting out many demons out of a man who was living in the country of the Gadarenes, located in the Gentile controlled area on the eastern shore of the Sea of Galilee (Matthew 8:28-34; Mark 5:1-20; Luke 8:26-39).

Hundreds of years before Jesus came, the prophet Isaiah wrote about the spiritual darkness and wickedness that Jesus would encounter in this region (Isaiah 8:19-9:2). As you read the fifth chapter of Mark, notice that this demon possessed man was naked and violent. His conscience was silenced and the demons had enslaved him so they could abuse him, while also using him for their own personal wicked gratification. When Jesus healed the man controlled by these demons, he clothed himself and soon sat at the feet of Jesus in worship. Jesus had restored the man to his right frame of mind. From this text we can observe that the demonic influence in this man's life caused him to not be ashamed of his nudity. Dr. Merrill Unger, in his excellent book, *Demons in the World Today*, writes, "Men and women who abandon themselves to immorality reach a point when God gives them up, in the sense of restraining Satan and demonic power from them, so that they are abandoned to the degrading depths of immorality and are shamelessly reduced to actions that even animals avoid. ... In such moral decay the 'unclean spirit' takes possession of the sinner to gratify his senses through every type of unclean pleasure. This is apparently why a demoniac often desires to live in a state of nudity and harbors licentious thoughts (Luke 8:27). When men disobey the moral laws of God, especially the law of loving and honoring their Creator, they choose the depraved way of Satan and demons. ... Some unsaved people who live a balanced moral life are only mildly influenced by demonic spirits, while others, who flout

God's moral laws, are severely influenced to the point of subjection. ... When the moral law of God is persistently and flagrantly disregarded, demon influence may merge into demon subjection. The sinner becomes the slave of the demon." [1] I believe the Bible teaches that true believers in Christ may be oppressed by demons, but cannot fall under demon possession. Demons cannot live where the Holy Spirit dwells.

Dr. Unger's observation should blare out a clear and resounding loud warning to anyone who is enslaved by pornography. The Bible teaches that demons appeal to the sinful desires of people by appealing to their sensual appetites (James 3:15). Demons desire to fill their sinful cravings through a human subject. Demons are roaming the earth looking for individuals to enslave. They are looking for a person that will become their puppet. They want a person who has a conscience that has been seared (1 Timothy 4:1-2). This person will have no inhibitions. Therefore, the demons will be able to use their body and mind to accomplish hell's agenda, while destroying their victim.

According to the Bible, since the fall of man in the Garden of Eden, nudity produces shame in the conscience of man (Genesis 3:7). When this shame is replaced by lust and acceptance, it is an indication that those individuals are on the road to the spiritual point of no return. When men and woman can joyfully and shamelessly pose nude, it is an indication they are being influenced by demons. Those who traffic porn sites are actually flirting with demons. This is not only dangerous, it ultimately can be eternally damning! This is why a caring God commands us, "Flee also youthful lust: but follow righteousness, faith, love, peace with them that call on the Lord out of a pure heart" (2 Timothy 2:22).

What should a person do that is struggling with a porn addiction?

First, you must honestly confess your sin to God and cry out to Him for His forgiveness and mercy. Read 1 John 1:8-10. Jesus is the only one who can set you free from the slave monster of porn and the demons who are attempting to damn your soul. (John 8:34, 36) This is a spiritual war that is going on in your soul. Read Galatians 5:16-21.

God wants to save you. Satan wants to destroy you. Will you choose life or death?

Control your thoughts by controlling your senses. The victory over porn begins with controlling your thoughts (James 1:14-15). In order to accomplish this, you must make wise choices concerning what you look at, hear, and what you experience. Read Proverbs 4:23-27. Do not place yourself in a position of temptation. This may require drastic measures. While speaking about sexual lust, Jesus said, "And if thy right eye offend thee, pluck it out, and cast it from thee: for it is profitable for thee that one of thy members [of your body] should perish, and not that thy whole body should be cast into hell" (Matthew 5:29). You must not only avoid hard-core porn, but even what is being labeled as "soft porn" (women who are seductively and scantily dressed). All forms of porn must be avoided at any cost. Our American culture is openly embracing all forms of sensuality and immorality. Our government has given its approval. Public schools are teaching kids how to have "safe" sex. The media industry promotes it because it sells their products. This is why I have chosen not to watch much television. I will also not visit a beach without my wife at my side. I hate rock music and country music because it is filled with wickedness. If you do not control your eyes and ears then you will lose the battle of the war for your soul! The price for victory is high. However, the price of failure is even greater!

Feed your conscience the Word of God. I cannot overstress the importance of guarding and feeding our conscience. If a person is to have victory over any sin, including porn, they must have a powerful conscience that will enable the Holy Spirit to bring immediate warning, fear, and shame as they face the temptation to commit sin. The conscience, just like a muscle, does not become weak or strong in matter of days.

To experience victory over porn, a person must commit to a disciplined lifestyle of Scripture memorization and meditation. Select passages in the Bible that deal with the sin of sexual immorality and begin to read them, mediate upon them, and commit them to memory.

If you are not willing to do this, you will fail! Porn will continue to be a cruel master that will dominate your life and your soul will be damned. We are not saved by our works, but our lifestyle certainly reveals the spiritual condition of our soul. Read 1 John 1:1-10 and 3:4-10. Real believers cannot continually have a lifestyle of rebellion against God and live in wickedness. Please ask yourself: "Have I ever had a real relationship with God?" I urge you to read the little biblical book of 1 John. It has been written so that every person can examine his life to know if he is really saved. 1 John 5:13 says, "These things have I written to unto you that believe on the name of the Son of God: that ye may know that ye have eternal life." I have written a 57-page booklet on "How to Know you are Saved." Contact our ministry to obtain a copy of this booklet.

You must desire to be righteous. At the heart of turning from any sin is genuine biblical repentance. Repentance, motivated by guilt and sorrow, is a change in mind that leads to a change in action (lifestyle). Repentance always means you are turning away from sin and turning to God. You are turning from self and yielding to the Holy Spirit. You are turning from sin to righteousness. In order for this to take place, there needs to be a fear and hatred for sin and a love and desire for righteousness (to be holy- morally pure). This can only happen when you walk in the Spirit and fill your mind with the Word of God (Galatians 5:16 -21). In his great Sermon on the Mount, Jesus said, "Blessed are they which do hunger and thirst after righteousness: for they shall be filled" (Matthew 5:6). Hebrews 12:14 declares, "Follow peace with all men, and holiness, without which no man shall see the Lord."

Get married if you struggle with this. In 1 Corinthians 7:9, God admonishes the single person who is struggling with sexual self-control to get married. It is better to marry and enjoy sex with your spouse than to remain single and suffer the consequences of struggling to control burning sexual desires that have no God-honoring way to be expressed. Just like eating, sex is pleasurable. However, the Bible condemns gluttony. Even so, God-given sexual appetites must be controlled in the way that God has ordained - in the intimacy of a biblical marital relationship.

<u>Warning</u>: There is a great price to pay when you strive to be morally pure in a pornographic, sexually immoral culture. You will be perceived by the majority of the crowd as being strange or weird. It could cost you some friendships. Read Psalm 1. However, the consequence of following the culture and its immoral lifestyle has a greater consequence – eternal damnation.

CHAPTER 10

Striving for Moral Purity in a Sex-Crazy World

"Marriage is honorable in all, and the bed undefiled: but
whoremongers and adulterers God will judge."
Hebrews 13:4

THE MOST POWERFUL KING OF ISRAEL, SOLOMON,
once said: "There is no new thing under the sun" (Ecclesiastes
1:9). It is true that sexual immorality has been a part of our fallen
world from the very beginning. However, statistical data seem to
indicate that the craze for all forms of deviant sexual behavior
is running rampant around the world. For those of us who lived
before the sexual revolution in the turbulent 1960s in America, it is
abundantly clear that our nation is being saturated with sensuality
and immorality more than ever before. Here are several statistics
that prove this:

- "Approximately one-third of the entire population of the United
  States (110 million people) currently has a sexually transmitted
  disease according to the Centers for Disease Control and
  Prevention.
- Every single year, there are 20 million new STD [sexually
  transmitted disease] cases in America.

- America has the highest STD infection rate in the entire industrialized world.
- Americans in the 15 to 24-year-old age group account for about 50 percent of all new STD cases each year.
- According to one survey, 24 percent of all U.S. teens that have STDs say that they still have unprotected sex.
- According to a study conducted by the Centers for Disease Control and Prevention, approximately two-thirds of all Americans in the 15 to 24-year-old age bracket have engaged in oral sex.
- At this point, one out of every four teen girls in the U.S. has at least one sexually transmitted disease.
- According to the National Center for Missing and Exploited Children, there are 747,408 registered sex offenders in the United States.
- An astounding 30 percent of all Internet traffic now goes to adult websites.
- It has been estimated that 89 percent of all pornography is produced in the United States.
- In the United States today, more than half of all couples 'move in together' before they get married.
- For women under the age of 30 in the United States, more than half of all babies are being born out of wedlock." [1]

Does anyone care to remember Jesus said, "Whosoever looketh on a woman to lust after her hath committed adultery with her already in his heart"? (Matthew 5:28) Sensuality and immorality are the norm for these last days; just as they were when the Lord judged the entire world with a global flood in the days of Noah and when He destroyed Sodom and Gomorrah. When Jesus was asked about the signs of His coming He responded, "But as the days of Noah were, so shall also the coming of the Son of man be" (Matthew 24:37). A study of the culture of Noah's day, as revealed in Genesis 6, demonstrates global immorality was so common the Lord "saw that the wickedness of man was great in the earth, and that every imagination of the thoughts of his heart was only evil continually" (Genesis 6:5). This verse is a commentary on Noah's generation.

In Genesis 6:1-4 we are told that during the time of a global population explosion, men were looking upon women and saw they were "fair." The Hebrew word "fair" means they saw them as being "beautiful." The Bible tells us "the sons of God" were having sex with the "daughters of men" and the result was an offspring who were "giants" (Genesis 6:1-4).

The surface reading and consideration of these verses does not reveal the real story behind the days of Noah. The term "sons of God" is sometimes a reference in the Bible to angels (Job 1:6). But in this case, because of the wickedness associated with their activity, we are forced to conclude this is a reference to fallen angels – demons. In the days of Noah, demon possessed-men and women were motivated to commit lewd immoral acts with other men and women, creating a physical offspring who were "giants." The word "giant" in Hebrew means "fallen ones." In this case, the offspring of the immoral activity in Noah's day did not produce physical giants, but spiritually giant sinners. Therefore, this context demands that we conclude these sinful, immoral parents, who were being influenced by demons, were giving birth to children who were controlled by the same demons. Like their parents, they were grossly immoral. Like in our culture today, these great demon-possessed immoral people became the heroes of their time.

Luke also reminds the Bible reader the last days will be like the days of Lot in Sodom when "it rained fire and brimstone from heaven, and destroyed them all" (Luke 17:28-30). A study of Genesis 18-19 reveals God patiently waited until the sin of homosexuality had a firm grip upon the entire city of Sodom. When two angels from heaven entered Lot's house that fateful night, all of the men "compassed the house round, both old and young, all the people from every quarter" (Genesis 19:4). This militant homosexual crowd demanded Lot to deliver the two men to them so they could sexually abuse them throughout the night. They were planning to gang rape them! In Genesis 18:20, the Lord revealed the grief of His heart when He declared, "the cry of Sodom and Gomorrah is great, and … their sin is very grievous." Even after the angels supernaturally struck these men with blindness, "they wearied themselves to find the door" (Genesis 19:11). Apparently, even after divine judgment, they were still determined to enter Lot's house to carry out their lustful desires.

In a similar way, after three and one-half years of the harsh judgments of God during the future time of tribulation, in which at least one-half of the world's population will be killed (Revelation 6:8 and 9:15), those who survive will not want to give up their sexual immorality (Revelation 9:21). Note that the immorality of those living in the tribulation will be directly connected to demon worship, violence, the occult (which includes mind-altering drugs), and theft (Revelation 9:20-21). Therefore, we must conclude our world today is globally running toward its appointment with the judgment of God in the last days!

In many ways, the U.S. is inundating the world with its immorality as we export our rock music, movies, and pornography to the nations of the world. As you travel to other nations, you can hear this godless music and see the sensual fashions that are permeating the world!

One must ask, "Where is the church in all of this mess? Where are the voices of the men of God who need to sound the warning to their spouses and children? "Where are all of the Sunday school teachers, youth workers and pastors who should be faithfully proclaiming what the Bible has to say about sex?" The church is to be salt and light in the midst of the spiritual darkness of a nation. However, statistics indicate many pastors and church members are morally no different than the world. Tragically, the church has become a part of the problem rather than a part of the solution to bring about a spiritual turning back to God! More than ever before, we need men of God who will proclaim and model moral purity in our homes, churches, communities, and nation!

In light of all of this, let us examine nine biblical imperatives that promote sexual purity:

1. We must fear God!

This is where everything in our lives must begin and end. Psalm 111:10 says, "The fear of the LORD is the beginning of wisdom." Proverbs 3:7 adds, "Be not wise in thine own eyes; fear the LORD, and depart from evil." Proverbs 16:6 declares it is the fear of God that causes men to "depart from evil." The word fear communicates we should be in awe of God and respectfully afraid of Him. Do you fear God? If not, why not? Is it because you do not know the Bible and believe what it teaches about the One who made you, watches you, and controls your next heartbeat and breath?

The Bible states, "the ways of man are before the eyes of the LORD, and he pondereth all his goings" (Proverbs 5:21). Are you aware God sees everything you do? Are you aware He knows your every thought? Do you realize God knows all about the motives that direct the desires of your heart? We can hide nothing from God! The Lord has declared, "Can any hide himself in secret places that I shall not see him? saith the LORD. Do not I fill heaven and earth? saith the LORD" (Jeremiah 23:24). Your spouse may not see you while you are flirting with another person at work or looking at lurid pictures on the Internet. Your parents may not know you are engaging in sexual immorality. But God does – He knows all and sees all!

When the Old Testament patriarch Joseph was tempted by Potiphar's wife to have sex, he responded, "How then can I do this great wickedness, and sin against God?" (Genesis 39:9) When the moment of sexual temptation came to this godly man, he was not focusing upon the beauty of the woman or the opportunity for him to enjoy some forbidden physical pleasure. Instead, he was able to run away from this temptation because he loved and feared God! Pleasing God was more important to him than satisfying and gratifying his body for a fleeting moment.

If you are not in awe of Almighty God, then you are in deep trouble! You can learn to fear God by reading the Bible and constantly asking yourself as you read every verse, "What does this teach me about God?" Unfortunately, most people who call themselves Christians want to use the Bible to manipulate God, or play "Let's make a deal," so He will bless them. We should read the Bible to get to know God so we can live for Him and please Him. This is how real Christians live! For instance, this was the highest ambition of the apostle Paul, who exhorted all believers to follow his example (Philippians 3:7-17).

2. We must realize we are wicked and vulnerable to immorality!

Jesus taught that all sexual immorality comes from the heart of man (Matthew 15:19). We cannot blame anyone but ourselves. The Bible exposes the one who is at fault with these words, "Let no man say when he is tempted, I am tempted of God: for God cannot be tempted with evil, neither tempteth he any man. But every man is tempted when he is drawn away of his own lust, and enticed" (James 1:13-14). We want to avoid the truth that sexual immorality is a direct result of our sin nature. Please consider this, "Wherefore let him that thinketh he standeth take heed lest he fall. There hath no temptation taken you but such as is common to man" (1 Corinthians 10:12-13). Even godly King David fell into sexual sin and tried to cover it up with another sin (2 Samuel 11:1-27).

In essence, you may view yourself as a godly person, but you are a fool if you think you are immune from a particular sin, especially sexual immorality. If you ignore the Word of God and its teachings, you make yourself vulnerable to sin by letting your guard down. Every true believer is wise to agree with God that his own heart "is deceitful above all things, and desperately wicked: who can know it" (Jeremiah 17:9)? This was the testimony and experience of the apostle Paul's attitude toward his sinfulness. Read Romans 7:15-25.

3. We must feed our conscience the Bible and heed its warning concerning purity!

Our Creator has made every one of us with a built-in warning system for our soul – the conscience. This conscience either accuses us when we sin, or it excuses us when we are pleasing God (Romans 2:15). "The conscience, however, is not infallible. Nor is it a source of revelation about right or wrong. Its role is not to teach us moral and ethical ideals, but to hold us accountable to the highest standards of right and wrong we know. The conscience is informed by tradition as well as by truth, so the standards it holds us to are not necessarily biblical ones (1 Corin. 8:6-9)." [2]

The Bible – the written Word of God – holds the key to a conscience that promotes goodness and purity. We must be disciplined and feed our conscience the Word of God so that it will shame us, convict us, and bring guilt when we sin against God. This is what makes Psalm 119:11 work, "Thy word have I hid in mine heart [conscience], that I might not sin against thee." The Bible trains the conscience toward godliness and moral purity. While we feed the conscience the standard of God, we must at the same time guard it. Immorality defiles and contaminates the conscience (Titus 1:15).

We live in a society where most people foolishly think they can be harmlessly exposed to all kinds of violence and perversion. People foolishly think they can be entertained by sin and not be affected by it. But a day will come in eternity when God will judge the damning role television and the entertainment industry has had on our society. Read Proverbs 4:23-27. In this text, God warns us to guard our minds by limiting what goes through the gates of our ears, eyes, and other senses. We need to daily practice Psalm 101:3, "I will set no wicked thing before mine eyes." In other words, God is telling us to make a covenant with our eyes.

Statistics indicate that members of our churches are living just like the world because they have weak consciences. They are not hiding God's Word in their hearts and they are not refraining from exposure to the immoral filth of the world. How can we expect anything else?

4. We must understand where the road of sexual immorality begins.

A person generally does not just wake up one morning and decide to commit an act of sexual immorality. It always starts with lust – a sinful desire in his heart. James 1:15 tells it all: "Then when lust hath conceived, it bringeth forth sin: and sin, when it is finished, bringeth forth death"

(James 1:15). The root of every immoral act can be traced back to a gaze that turned into a lustful desire. This desire breeds immoral meditation, which eventually leads to action to carry out powerful inner cravings. The Bible repeatedly warns us to not underestimate the controlling power of sexual lust. Proverbs 6:27-29 illustrates that it's like playing with fire. No one has been physically created so that they can carry fire around in their pocket. Likewise, we have not been spiritually created to play around with mental immorality!

The Bible repeatedly sounds the alarm that looking at nudity or a scantly-dressed woman is dangerous (Proverbs 6:25-26 and 7:6-27). All sin is addictive and pornography is not an exception! Don't look and lust. Like all other sin, it controls. It destroys. It kills. Sexual lust and immorality bind their victim "with the cords of his sins" (Proverbs 5:22). Jesus said, "Whosoever commits sin [keeps on practicing a sin] is the servant [slave] of sin. ... If the Son therefore shall make you free, ye shall be free indeed" (John 8:34, 36).

5. We must remind ourselves where the road of immorality ends!

All sin is deceptive. It always looks good and inviting. It promises pleasure but never tells you where it always leads. God's warning about the results of sexual immorality reverberates throughout the Holy Scriptures. Proverbs 6:32 sounds God's trumpet alarm, "But whoso committeth adultery with a woman lacketh understanding: he that doeth it <u>destroyeth his own soul</u>." God attempts to write this message of warning upon our hearts by giving us many colorful and graphic pictures of the tragic result of immorality. When a person involves himself in sexual immorality, he becomes a "shipwreck" (1 Timothy 1:19). He is like an ox being led to the slaughter (Proverbs 7:22). A person pursuing sexual immorality is compared to a fool who is being led "to the correction of the stocks" (Proverbs 7:22). Tragically, the person searching for an immoral encounter is compared to a bird that is hurrying into a trap that will take its life (Proverbs 7:23). Illustrating the ultimate eternal outcome of this person, the Bible declares he has entered the door of the house of death that leads to hell (Proverbs 7:24-27)!

The deceptiveness of sin focuses our attention only upon the pleasure offered by sin. All sin brings pleasure "for a season" (Hebrews 11:25). However, the sinful road that advertises pleasure on its many billboards ultimately leads its victims around a blind curve that plunges them into the valley of death. Sexual immorality brings many painful and chilling effects. Deadly diseases are spread. Homes are broken. Lives are destroyed. People's consciences are desensitized. Abusive behavior occurs. Lives become unfulfilled, bringing dissatisfaction. Lifestyles become more selfish. And most tragically, our fellowship with a holy God is disrupted. Like all other sin, sexual immorality never delivers what it promises.

6. We must remind ourselves we are to be different from this sensual world!

We live in a world where sensuality has become the model and desire of many people around us. Millions of Americans have idols and heroes that are immoral people who flaunt their sensuality. Consequently, millions of men and women want to look sexy. They have bought into the mindset and lifestyle that are being promoted in all of the entertainment and advertisement industries in our sensual culture.

Statistics report that men of all ages are committing mental adultery many times each day. We are living in a culture wallowing in a selfish and sensual lifestyle, living for a few brief moments of self-gratification. The truth detailed about the last days in 2 Timothy 3:1-7 is a commentary on our age. This text reports that the last days will be dangerous because of the self-centeredness of the age that will culminate in various forms of hatred, violence, deception, lawlessness, and immorality. These people are "ever learning, and never able to come to the knowledge of the truth" (2 Timothy 3.7).

As believers in Jesus Christ we must daily remind ourselves God has called us to be holy. God commands us, "Be ye holy; for I am holy" (1 Peter 1:16). Our ultimate aim is to be like Christ. Therefore, there is no room for sensuality or immorality in the mind or body of the believer!

In the apostle Paul's day, the Corinthian believers were living in one of the most flagrant sensual cultures in the ancient Roman world. The city of Corinth was one of the most important and influential cities of its time. It was located in a strategic position to attract commercial traffic from all over the ancient world. It was at the base of a mountain on which was located the temple of Venus, the Greek goddess of love. This temple was known all over the ancient world for its 1,000 beautiful temple prostitutes, dedicated to leading the worship of Venus by providing their immoral services in honor of this goddess of love.

All of these factors ultimately played a part in Corinth becoming one of the most prolific sensual and immoral playgrounds of the ancient world. Consequently, Corinth became a magnet for homosexuality and all other forms of deviant sexual behavior. The Lord called the apostle Paul to graciously establish a church in this wicked city. During his ministry, Paul wrote several letters to the believers at Corinth, exhorting them concerning moral purity. In one of these letters, he reminded them they had been purchased by Jesus Christ and belonged physically and spiritually to Him. As believers in Jesus Christ, we are to view our bodies as the temple of the Holy Spirit. Therefore, we should not have any part in sexual immorality which would defile our body, and bring shame upon our Holy Lord Jesus (1 Corinthians 6:15-20).

7. We must not forget the role of Satan and his demons in immorality!

An examination of several Biblical texts reveals that Satan and his demons have a long history of involvement with immorality! Satan and his minions played a major role in the sexual immorality that manifested itself in the days preceding the global flood in Noah's time. According to the context of Genesis 6:1-13, demons promote moral corruption, wickedness, and violence in the global rebellion against their Creator. The apostle Peter (2 Peter 2:4-5) and Jude (Jude 6-7) confirm this observation. Demons promote nudity and a lack of moral shame in individuals. Note that the demon-possessed man that was living in the tombs in Luke 8 was naked (verse 27) and he showed no shame as he appeared before others.

According to 1 Timothy 4:1-2, demonic influence plays some part in numbing people's consciences. Thus, such things as nudity and immorality do not bring guilt, shame, or remorse. It is most revealing to note that after Jesus cast the demons out of the man in Luke 8 there was a dramatic change in his life. When the people of his community looked at him after the demons were cast out, they observed He was "sitting at the feet of Jesus, clothed, and in his right mind" (Luke 8:35). When the demons were gone, his spiritual eyes were opened and his conscience was restored so that his shame caused him to clothe himself.

It is important that all servants of God take note that Satan has many weapons in his arsenal to tempt God's people to fall into sin. Satan's goal is for God's children to bring disgrace to our Lord (Ephesians 6:10-18). On one occasion, the Lord reminded the apostle Peter. "Satan hath desired to have you, that he may sift you as wheat" (Luke 22:31). The Bible pulls back the curtain of the spirit world to reveal that Satan loves to sexually tempt the person whose spouse is not meeting their sexual needs (1 Corinthians 7:2-5).

The prevalence of sexual immorality among pastors and professing believers is all too common in these last days. We would do well to heed that the promotion of all forms of illicit sexual activity are a key part of demons' daily agenda. Remember, the Bible tells us this world system we live in has Satan as its prince and is in direct opposition to God (John 12:31). We should wake up and realize that demonic influence is directly related to all forms of illicit sex. Yes, our minds tell us that illicit sex can bring pleasure and enjoyment. But when we act on our desires, Satan's demons laugh because they know their deceptive and wicked forms of deception have worked. Demons, just like their master, Satan, want to destroy marriages. They want to destroy personal lives. They want to destroy the testimonies of Christians in churches. They especially aim to destroy the spiritual light in churches that expose their hellish wickedness and darkness.

Satan's power, coupled with our own sin nature can only be resisted with a greater power – the power of God. We must fight this spiritual warfare with God's armor, not ours! "For we wrestle not against flesh and blood, but against principalities, against powers, against the rulers of the darkness of this world, against spiritual wickedness in high places. Wherefore take unto you the whole armor of God, that ye may be able to withstand in the evil day, and having done all, to stand" (Ephesians 6:12-13).

The biblical analogy of putting on the armor defends us against the fiery darts of Satan. Believers are exhorted to put on "the breastplate of righteousness" (Ephesians 6:14). In biblical times, the Roman soldier knew how important the breastplate was. It protected the vital organs in his chest. The chest was the primary target of his enemy! Likewise, when Satan tempts us with illicit sensual pleasure, he is aiming for our spiritual heart! Think about that! Putting on the breastplate of righteousness means that we must know and practice God's righteous standards of morality! We should long for holiness and moral purity in our lives, in our families, and in our churches. This will be reflected in how we dress, what we read, what television programs we watch, what kind of music we listen to, what places we visit on the Internet, and what we desire in our hearts!

8. We must practice the biblical imperative to RUN from sexual temptation!

Sexual temptation is powerful. It has destroyed many in its path. It has destroyed the lives of many good people. In response to defending oneself against sexual temptation, the Bible gives one simple and powerful exhortation – RUN! When you see something that is sexually tempting, do not keep looking or it will be too late. The Bible exhorts us to "flee fornication" (1 Corinthians 6:18). We must run from "youthful lusts" (2 Timothy 2:22). Mentally and physically we must remove ourselves from the presence of sexual temptation. A few seconds of lusting can lead to a lifetime of tragedy and disappointment.

Once again, let us consider that the Lord has given us a powerful example of this exhortation in the life of the Old Testament patriarch Joseph. It is apparent that even at an early age the hand of the Lord was upon Joseph. Through his dreams, God had revealed to Joseph that He had a very special assignment for him. After he was sold into slavery by his brothers, Joseph was taken to Egypt. Ultimately, he was purchased by Potiphar, who was an officer of Pharaoh. In spite of his circumstances, God was with Joseph. Even those around him noted that "the LORD was with him" (Genesis 39:3). As Joseph served the Lord and his master, Potiphar, a very serious temptation took place in his young life. The Bible informs us that Potiphar's wife had eyes for Joseph. She began to constantly bagger him to have sex with her. Joseph was in a difficult position. He had to be in her presence in the process of performing his daily tasks for his master. The Bible tells us on one occasion when Potiphar's wife approached him to have sex with her, Joseph replied by stating he could not do that because it was "wicked," and it would be a sin against her husband, and it would be a sin against God (Genesis 39:8-9). Finally, one day Potiphar's wife physically grabbed Joseph by his clothing and insisted that he have sex with her. The Bible tells us that Joseph ran out the house and removed himself from the temptation.

Joseph did what we all are exhorted to do in the face of immediate sexual temptation – run! The fact that Joseph ran away from this temptation was because he was not focusing upon himself or the sexual pleasure that was before him. He was thinking about His God and knew if he did not flee he would sin against God and his master.

The only people who can run away from sexual temptation are those who are not focused upon themselves or the immediate sexual gratification before them. Like Joseph, we must have a clear mind set of the consequences of sexual immorality. We must be prepared to run when temptation comes. We only have a few seconds to make that decision. If we linger, we will lust. If we lust and linger we will fail God and fall into the trap Satan has set before us. Be prepared to run, both mentally and physically.

9. We must remember that in a moment we could be standing before our holy Judge!

Those who claim they are saved and are not living a holy and pure moral life, both mentally and physically, are not watching for the imminent coming of the Lord Jesus! The potential for our Rapture into the presence of our holy Lord Jesus at any moment should have a purifying effect upon us. "Beloved, now are we the sons of God, and it doth not yet appear what we shall be: but we know that, when he shall appear, we shall be like him; for we shall see him as he is, And every man that hath this hope in him purifieth himself even as he is pure" (1 John 3:2-3). The apostle Paul concluded his life with these words, "I have fought a good fight, I have finished my course, I have kept the faith: Henceforth there is laid up for me a crown of righteousness, which the Lord, the righteous judge, shall give me at that day: and not to me only, but unto all them that love his appearing" (2 Timothy 4:7-8). Note that Paul connected personal, righteous living with those who were looking for Jesus' coming and expecting it at any moment.

It is obvious the world we live in today, along with many professing believers in the church, do not believe "the judge standeth before the door" (James 5:9). If they did, our world and our churches would not be tainted with sensuality, pornography, and immorality!

What can you do if you have fallen into the clutches of immorality? First, cry out to God for forgiveness (1 John 1:8-10). Begin to live a life of repentance. Turn away from sin and turn to Christ. Desire to "walk in the Spirit" (Galatians 5:16-21). Seek God's face and look expectantly each day for the coming of the Lord. Begin to saturate your conscience with biblical admonitions and warnings that are mentioned in this chapter. Recognize your weakness toward this sin and understand that this is spiritual warfare for your soul! Demons are using lurid sexual temptation to snare you into their deceptive and damning trap! Remember: A the person who yields to sexual temptation "destroyeth his own soul" (Proverbs 6:32). This is why Jesus stressed that sexual temptation requires a serious response. Read Matthew 5:28-30.

Biblical history and prophecy demonstrate that when a nation descends into the pits of immorality it has departed from the rock of life and salvation and has built its life upon the sands of sin that will destroy its people!

CHAPTER 11

Living in a Demonic Society

"Now the Spirit speaks expressly, that in the latter times
some shall depart from the faith, <u>giving heed to
seducing spirits, and doctrine of [demons]</u>; Speaking lies in
hypocrisy; having their conscience seared with a hot iron."
1 Timothy 4:1-2

A S I POUR OVER BIBLICAL HISTORY AND PROPHECIES
of the Bible, it is clear that when the collective conscience of a
society has been seared, demonic influence will escalate. Eventually,
demonic influence will pave the way for demonic possession. This leads
us to ask the following questions. What would it be like to live in a
demonic society? Has that day arrived? How can we be so sure? We
must turn to the Bible for the answers to these alarming and disturbing
questions.

The Bible tells us the end of this age will be a time of great demonic
influence on a global scale. With Satan as their leader, demons will strive
to take over the world and usher in a hellish kingdom of rebellion that
will seek to defeat God. Satan and his minions want to destroy God's
people and their ultimate goal is to thwart His eternal plans. This is
illustrated numerous times in the New Testament epistles and in the
Book of Revelation.

Satan's strategy to accomplish his ultimate objective has not changed much from the time of his fall from heaven. The Bible tells us that Satan was originally known as Lucifer, a beautiful and bright angel. Ultimately, he led a revolt against God in heaven and consequently fell from his position as a messenger and servant of God (see Isaiah 14:12-14). Since that time, his wicked schemes and objectives have not deviated. Therefore, we must learn from past history and apply what we learn so we can be aware of his wicked agenda.

The classic example of Satan's efforts to defeat God can be observed during the first coming of our Lord to this earth. During Jesus' first earthly visit, the gospels indicate Satan had collectively prepared his demons to defeat Jesus. Nevertheless, Jesus was fully aware of Satan's insidious agenda. He confronted Satan. He resisted his efforts. And, He defeated him! As He approached the cross, Jesus proclaimed, "Now is the judgment of this world; now shall the prince of this world be cast out" (John 12:31). This declaration by our Lord indicates Satan and his demons have already lost the war! They have been defeated – FOREVER! But this has not deterred their powerful efforts to thwart God's eternal plans. Satan and his demons are still acting in desperation, working to overthrow the One who has predicted, and will control, their ultimate doom!

Perhaps one of the best examples of Jesus' confrontation with demons during His earthly ministry is found in Luke 8:26-39. Read this passage before continuing with this chapter.

To understand this text, you must first observe the historical setting for our Lord's confrontation with demons. Up to this point in time, Jesus had almost exclusively ministered to the Jewish people (who were the major focus of His entire earthly ministry- see Matthew 10:5-6). With a few exceptions, He moved about only in areas where Jewish people lived. Nonetheless, on this occasion He took His disciples to the eastern side of the Sea of Galilee to a district that was strictly off limits for the Jewish people in His day! This domain was a Gentile area given over to the worship of pagan gods and idols of the Greeks. The Lord had commanded the Jews to exclusively worship Him as the One and only true God (see Exodus 20:3-6). Therefore, this area was off limits because of the pagan idolatry.

Furthermore, this area was a place where these Gentiles raised pigs, some of which were raised to be sacrifices to their Greek gods. For the Jews, pigs were considered to be unclean animals. This meant that they were forbidden to raise them or eat them. Clearly, this area was considered unclean to the Jewish people.

Jesus had a purpose for taking His disciples into this pagan Gentile stronghold. I believe the Bible gives us at least five reasons why Jesus did this.

First, he wanted to prepare them for the Great Commission. After His earthly ministry was complete, they would be commanded to take the gospel to "all nations" (Matthew 28:19). A study of the book of Acts reveals that the Holy Spirit would lead the disciples into many countries deeply immersed in the same pagan idolatry that was prevalent on the eastern shores of the Sea of Galilee.

Secondly, Jesus wanted to prepare His disciples for spiritual warfare. He knew that after He returned to His Father in heaven that Satan's wrath would be directed upon His disciples and their followers.

Third, Jesus wanted His disciples to see that in the ongoing conflict between heaven and hell, He has all power over Satan and his demons. The disciples had witnessed many miracles by Jesus where He cast the demons out (see Mark 1:32-34). However, in Luke 8, Jesus' encounter with another demon possessed man gives us an unusual display of the fear and respect that demons have for the power of God.

Fourthly, Jesus brought His disciples to this heathen land to save a pagan man, who seemingly could not be freed from the evil vices of demons. The gospels tell us that even this pagan society was fearful of this man's bizarre and violent behavior. This encounter would demonstrate to Jesus' disciples that His power to save sinners has no limits. He can save and set free those who are masterfully controlled by the powers of hell.

Lastly, I believe Jesus brought His disciples to this district to reveal the nature of a demonic society. The abnormal and destructive behavior of this man was the direct result of the "many demons" who were living in him (see Luke 8:30). After he was set free from the presence and power of these demons, his bizarre and violent behavior disappeared (see Luke 8:35). Therefore, we can conclude Jesus wanted His disciples to witness first-hand the nature of a person and society who were controlled by demons. The Holy Spirit has given us this account in three of the four gospels, providing us with a biblical illustration of a demonic society.

Before we proceed with an examination of this example of a demonic society, we need to answer a few questions. What are demons? What is the goal of demons? And, how do demons influence people?

Demons are not the direct creation of God. According to God's perfect and holy nature, He cannot create evil. In the beginning, everything God created was "good" (see Genesis 1). Lucifer (the original name for Satan) was created by God as a very powerful, intelligent, and talented good angel (Ezekiel 28:13-19). Ultimately his powerful position among all the angels led him to become filled with pride (see Isaiah 14:12-14). As a result, he led a rebellion in heaven against God. He successfully persuaded one-third of all the good angels (see Revelation 12:4) to follow his rebellion. These fallen angels are called demons, or unclean spirits. The Bible teaches that most demons are free to roam about the earth to help Satan in his rebellion against God. But a few of the most evil, wicked, violent, and rebellious of these demons are currently "reserved in everlasting chains under darkness unto the judgment of the great day" (Jude 6). This means these evil angels have been supernaturally restrained by God since the time of their personal rebellion against Him. The Bible teaches that our Lord is sovereign over all His creation, even to the extent that Satan and his demons are not free to do <u>all</u> that they want to do (for example see Job 1:12 and 2:6).

When Jesus confronted the demons controlling the violent man in Luke 8, they were afraid Jesus would force them to join their evil companions in the God-appointed prison. The demons pleaded with Jesus "that he would not command them to go out into the deep" (Luke 8:31). The word "deep" refers to "the abyss," the same place where the restrained evil angels are imprisoned. Instead of commanding them to prison, He granted the demons' request to enter the pigs feeding on the hillside. This allowed the disciples and others present to witness the manifesting presence of demons and their destructive powers. Jesus clearly exposed the demons' evil nature and intent to all who were there!

Satan and his demons are on a relentless march to destroy everything that is good and precious to God. Satan and his wicked army are working to develop a system that will support their rebellion against their effort to overthrow the Lord. Demons want to elevate Satan and themselves as the superpower of the supernatural world. They want people to worship them and participate in their rebellion against God.

The focus of their rebellion is the control of the crown of God's creation – man. Their objective is to control man and use him as a rebel against God. The Bible teaches that as a result of man's fall in the Garden of Eden, all of mankind is naturally open to the powerful influence of Satan. Satan and his demons do all they can to keep a sinner blind to the truth of God that would bring him to salvation (see 2 Corinthians 4:4). When a person is saved, he is "delivered from the power of darkness" (Colossians 1:13). However, when a person becomes a child of God, he becomes the enemy of Satan, and the satanic warfare intensifies and escalates. In Ephesians 6:10-20, the apostle Paul reminded the believers living in the ancient city of Ephesus they were engaged in a real and brutal war with the demonic world on a daily basis. Having visited the remains of this ancient city and viewed its wicked and immoral culture, I can better understand the reality of Paul's warning to these believers. The culture of Ephesus was deeply immersed in pagan idolatry and gross exaggerations of immorality. The demons had many opportunities to tempt the believers to fulfill the lusts of the flesh.

Demons attempt to control people by influencing the way they think. Proverbs 23:7 says, "For as he thinketh in his heart [mind], so is he." Demons know that if they can influence the way a person thinks, they can change who that person is.

Merrill F. Unger writes, "Bondage to demonic forces can be of varying degrees, as can yieldedness to God and control by the Holy Spirit. ... Some unsaved people who live a balanced moral life are only mildly influenced by demonic spirits, while others, who flout God's moral laws, are severely influenced to the point of subjection. Others are so dominated that they are oppressed and tormented, and some are completely possessed by evil spirits. ... When the moral law of God is persistently and flagrantly disregarded, demon influence may merge into demon subjection. The sinner then becomes the slave of the demon." [1]

As the Scriptures testify, demons can actually take up residence inside of a person's body and control their mind and body. A possessed person becomes a powerful tool of demons in the physical realm to oppose God and promote the "doctrine of [demons]" (1 Timothy 4:1).

We must be careful to not arrive at the conclusion that all sin is a direct or indirect result of demonic influence. The Bible teaches that man's sin is the direct result of his own personal sin nature and choice. James 1:14 says, "...every man is tempted, when he is drawn away of his own lust, and enticed." Jesus made this very clear when He said, "For from within, out of the heart of men, proceed evil thoughts, adulteries, fornications, murders, thefts, covetousness, wickedness, deceit, lasciviousness, an evil eye, blasphemy, pride, foolishness: All these evil things come from within, and defile the man" (Mark 7:21-23).

However, the Bible clearly teaches that a person loses control of his thoughts and actions when he is possessed by demons. In essence, he becomes a pawn and a direct tool of the forces of darkness!

Demons are actively roaming the earth. They are looking for a person or society with high levels of wickedness, violence, rebellion, and immorality. Demons want to invade such a culture and take its form of wickedness to a heightened level to promote the cause of Satan. Demon oppression then becomes demon possession!

I would suggest there are three distinct stages a society experiences as it degenerates from being a "good" society to becoming an "evil" one. In stage one, a society is predominately a good society, due to a powerful influence of a godly remnant of believers, who act as a restraining influence. With little demonic influence present, such a society honors and respects God. The society also respects His servants, and His Word. This society is firmly built upon the moral laws of God. This is a society, where the Holy Spirit is at work, and some men are <u>seeking</u> God. This stage represents the earlier years in American history.

When such a society degenerates to the next level, there will be a growing demonic influence. The society in stage two will not be predominately good or evil. To use the language of the Bible, they will become "lukewarm" (Revelation 3:16). The community of believers will become like the world and lose much of its ability to restrain sin in that society. In this state of confusion, people begin to play with sin. They lose their sense of honor or respect God. They also lose their respect for His servants, or His Word. This is a society that merely <u>tolerates</u> God! This stage represents America from the 1950s to 2000.

The final stage is the ultimate goal of Satan and his forces of evil. Such a society becomes demonic, meaning it is controlled by Satan and his demons. It is an "evil" society. Churches are collectively filled with unbelievers. Consequently, there is very little restraining influence remaining in this society, thus people become openly militant and defiant in their sinful lifestyles. This is a society that is <u>resisting</u> God! It is at this level demons control a society and use it in their attack upon God and His creation. This is the stage that represents America's culture since 2000.

It is quite apparent the U.S. is very rapidly spiraling into this final phase and is becoming a demonic society. In light of the prophetic Scripture, this is a significant development. Among all of the nations in the world today, the two that are hated the most are Israel and the U.S. In a limited sense, these are the last two nations founded upon Judeo-Christian values. Our great nation will eventually reach the final stage of becoming a demonic society. When this occurs, it will signal to the world that the final confrontation between God and Satan is near. These final days are spelled out in the prophetic texts of the Word of God!

The prophetic Scripture reveals that when the end of the age comes, the world will have evolved into a cultural and spiritual climate that will promote demonic control. This is precisely what happened in the days of Noah (see Genesis 6:1-13 and 2 Peter 2:4-5).

When Jesus took His disciples to the eastern shores of the Sea of

Galilee, He wanted them to see the power and nature of Satan's work in a society that was open to demonic possession. Turn to Luke 8:26-39 and examine what the disciples observed during this valuable lesson from our Lord.

Observation #1 about the nature of a demonic society: Pluralistic societies worship Satan's many gods as the first step toward a demonic society (Luke 8:26).

Luke first mentions the geographical setting of Jesus' confrontation with the man possessed by demons. It was in "the country of the Gadarenes, which is over against Galilee" (verse 26). As was mentioned previously, this was a totally pagan, Gentile area that was given over to the worship of Greek gods. These people were devoted to their religious worship of these gods. Furthermore, it should be noted this was a society void of any biblical revelation about the one and only true God of the Bible!

Satan's ultimate objective is to deceive us so mankind will worship him, rather than God. When Satan tempted Jesus to worship him, Jesus rebuked him and unveiled his deceptive agenda when He said, "Thou shalt worship the Lord thy God, and him only shalt thou serve" (Matthew 4:10). Jesus was informing Satan He knew his real objective was to have the Son of God serve him. Satan knows man will serve whom or what he worships. This is an important truth we all must grasp. Worshipping the Lord, and Him alone, is the highest priority and commandment given to man (see Exodus 20:3-6). Out of worship flows everything else in the Christian life!

There are no other true gods! The God of the Bible is the one and only true God. Through the prophet Isaiah the Lord continually rebuked Israel for their worship of idols and other gods. He said, "I am the LORD, and there is none else, there is no God beside me..." (Isaiah 45:5; see also 45:6, 18, 21-22 and 46:9-11).

The Bible reveals that all other gods and idols are the manifestation and promotion of demons (see Deuteronomy 32:17 and 1 Corinthians 10:20). When people worship anyone else but the God of the Bible, they are worshipping demons! When they worship these demons they will serve them, and their lifestyle will not reflect the holy nature and character of the God of the Bible. When Jesus warned His disciples about the false prophets that promote these false gods, He revealed they would be known by their godless lifestyle (see Matthew 7:15-20).

Therefore, Satan's first objective in the creation of a demonic society is to promote a pluralistic society. [A pluralistic society is one that attempts to worship many gods or idols, including the God of the Bible.] Once he can accomplish this objective, he knows people will be in a state of spiritual confusion. Then, he can continue his masterfully deceptive schemes and move them away from the worship of the God of the Bible altogether. When people are worshipping Satan and his false gods through these demonic manifestations, they will be serving him and they will become more open to demonic possession.

It is no coincidence that false religions are exploding in the U.S. and around the world. We have been warned this would occur. "Now the Spirit speaketh expressly, that in the latter times some shall depart from the faith, giving heed to seducing spirits and doctrines of devils [demons] ..." (1 Timothy 4:1). Satan and his demons know they are not welcomed in a society that exclusively worships the God of the Bible.

In the last few decades, the U.S. has become a very pluralistic society. We are being told we need to be very tolerant and open-minded to other religions and peoples' sinful lifestyles. Have you noticed all of the bumper stickers on cars calling for "coexistence"? Have you noticed that the symbol for Islam, the crescent moon, is first emblem on this bumper sticker? Also, have you observed that the symbol for Christianity, the cross, is the last emblem on this bumper sticker? The message these people are parading across America is that we need to be more tolerant when it comes to religion. From their deceptive perspective, all religions lead to heaven. However, in reality, these people tolerate Islam and are intolerant of evangelical Christianity.

The Bible leaves no room for such compromise. There is only one Bible and only one Savior! Jesus said, "I am the way, the truth, and the life; no man cometh unto the Father, but by me" (John 14:6; see also Acts 4:12 and 1 Timothy 2:5). At this hour, there are many voices in our nation proclaiming there are many ways to heaven. Who is lying? The Bible has proved it is always completely reliable! The declarations of men that do not agree with the Bible are not true. "If we receive the witness of men, the witness of God is greater; for this is the witness of God which he hath testified of his Son. He that believeth on the Son of God hath the witness in himself; he that believeth not God hath made him a liar; because he believeth not the record that God gave of his Son" (1 John 5:9-10).

Observation #2 about the demonic nature of a society: Demonic activity flourishes in a culture that embraces nudity, sexual immorality, and brutal violence (Luke 8:27).

When Jesus and His disciples arrived on the eastern shores of the Sea of Galilee, they immediately encountered a demon-possessed man who was naked and violent (see Luke 8:26-27 and Matthew 8:28). It is clear from the text this man's activity was not the result of some type of mental illness. After the demons were cast out of the man, he was "clothed and in his right mind" (Luke 8:35). Thus, we are forced to believe his nudity and violence were the result of the demons' control over him.

Bible history and prophecy demonstrate that demon possession is attached to nudity, immorality, and violence (see Genesis 6:1-13; Acts 19:14-16; and Revelation 9:20-21). Merrill F. Unger observes, "Men and women who abandon themselves to immorality reach a point when God gives them up, in the sense of restraining Satan and demonic power from them, so that they are abandoned to the degrading depths of immorality and are shamelessly reduced to actions that even animals avoid (Romans 1:26-32; Revelation 9:20-21).

"In such moral decay the 'unclean spirit' takes possession of the sinner to gratify his senses through every type of unclean pleasure. This is apparently why a demoniac often desires to live in a state of nudity and harbors licentious thoughts (Luke 8:27). When men disobey the moral laws of God, especially the law of loving and honoring their Creator, they choose the depraved way of Satan and demons." [2]

In 1 Timothy 4:1-2, the Apostle Paul warned that the last days would be filled with those who are "giving heed to seducing spirits," whose conscience will be "seared with a hot iron." In essence, the Holy Spirit is warning us that the last days will be filled with people who have a numbed conscience. They will suffer from a significant loss of shame, guilt, and remorse. This is the very beginning point of repentance in the human heart. When the Holy Spirit leads a person to repent of his sins, He brings him to a place of brokenness that is rooted in shame, guilt, and remorse (see 2 Corinthians 7:10).

Demons are looking for subjects with a spiritual point of numbness. Demons know they can control these people. Our society is filled with these kinds of people who participate in pornography, immorality, violence, and many other types of wickedness. This is a society ripe for demon possession.

Observation #3 about the nature of a demonic society: The mark of a demonic society is demonic doctrine- the inversion of God's truth [right and wrong] (Luke 8:27).

The gospel accounts of Jesus' confrontation with the demon possessed man report he was living in the tombs with the dead and was "cutting himself with stones" (Mark 5:5). It is evident these demons took over the man's mind and body to the point where they inverted reality, resulting behavior was totally abnormal.

Demons, like their master, do not care about their victims. Jesus compared Satan to a thief whose objective is to selfishly "steal, and to kill, and to destroy" (John 10:10). In Revelation 9:11, Satan is called "Abaddon" or "Apollyon," which means "destroyer." He delights in possessing men so that he inverts their normal fears. In the process, he leads them into self-inflicted pain. He causes them to embrace suffering and loneliness. Satan leads them to glorify death. Ultimately the devil tricks them into longing for eternal damnation.

To a community that flagrantly sins in the face of God, the prophet

Isaiah warned, "Woe unto them that call evil good, and good evil; that put darkness for light, and light for darkness; that put bitter for sweet, and sweet for bitter" (Isaiah 5:20)! The nations of Israel and Judah in Isaiah's day had reached a point of great spiritual rebellion against God. This was evidenced by their turning from God toward demons. Israel and Judah had turned to sorcery, witchcraft, and other forms of the occult (see Isaiah 8:19-22). The end result was divine judgment upon the people. They were driven even further into spiritual darkness (Isaiah 8:22). This means God gave them up and turned them over to demonic powers, bringing great pain, destruction, and death upon the people.

This spiritual darkness was most pronounced in the region surrounding the Sea of Galilee, belonging to the tribes of Zebulun and Naphtali (see Isaiah 9:1). However, Isaiah revealed that the Lord would "more grievously afflict" the Gentile area on the eastern shores of the Sea of Galilee with this demonic darkness (Isaiah 9:2). For more than 750 years these people were oppressed and possessed by powers of spiritual darkness. Jesus came and set them free. Isaiah wrote, "The people that walked in darkness have seen a great light: they that dwell in the land of the shadow of death, upon them hath the light shined" (Isaiah 9:2). Everywhere Jesus went, the demons trembled and bowed to His authority as He cast them out and set their victims free.

In 2 Timothy 3:1-9, the apostle Paul warned that the last days would be "perilous times." The Greek word translated "perilous" is found only one other time in the New Testament. In Matthew 8:28, the same word is used to describe the demon-possessed man who was "exceeding fierce." Therefore, the Holy Spirit is warning us that the last days will be filled with demon-possessed men and women who reject everything that is good and normal. They will hate God. They will hate their parents. In essence they will hate all that is good. At the same time, they will be filled with pride and speaks lies. They will be filled with wickedness and burn with an insatiable lust for pleasure.

One of the basic enemies and fears of man is death (see 1 Corinthians 15:26). When God told Adam of the consequences of disobedience if he ate the forbidden fruit in the Garden of Eden, He attached to it the sentence of death (see Genesis 2:17). This threat was to produce fear in Adam. Death, when people are thinking normally, is not attractive! [The only exception to this is when the child of God is about to enter into the presence of His Lord, and the Lord then removes the fear of death. Then, death becomes only the door through which we enter into our Lord's presence. The believer in Jesus Christ does not need to fear death because our Lord has conquered death for us (see 1 Corinthians 15:55-57 and Philippians 1:20- 24)].

The demon-possessed man in Luke 8 was living in the tombs among the dead. This is completely abnormal. Once again, we are forced to believe that the Bible conveys to us that demons had mentally inverted reality in this man's logic and thinking.

It is not by accident that we are observing a shocking rise in a morbid association of death in our global culture. The rock musicians of our age (who are immersed in the occult, mind-altering drugs, all types of bizarre behavior, immorality, and violence) have created and modeled this morbid association with death. To many in our culture today, these rock stars have literally become idols. They worship them and attempt to mimic them. With mindless and reckless abandonment, they have conformed to their message. In many cases, the lyrics of some of their songs promote suicide. Their message is a message from the destroyer, Satan! God does not promote suicide. Everything in the Bible proclaims that our God is a God of life. He blesses us with life. However, Satan is "a murderer" (see John 8:44). He is the one who promotes death! In Proverbs 8:35-36, the Lord declares, "For whoso findeth me findeth life, and shall obtain favor of the LORD. But he that sinneth against me wrongeth his own soul: <u>all they that hate me love death</u>."

The symbols of death are proudly displayed on clothing and automobiles throughout America. The entertainment industry glorifies murder, death, and violence. Video games that our kids play are filled with a demonic message that feeds their minds a constant diet of murder and violence. All of this is the promotion of demons!

Notice that this demonic man was cutting himself with the stones in the tombs. Historically, self-inflicted pain is associated with a diversity of ritualistic practices that are rooted in various religions and the occult (see 1 Kings 18:28). The Lord had commanded His chosen people, Israel, to not be like the other nations who were given over to the various practices of body piercing, cutting, and marking. In Leviticus 19:28, He commanded, "Ye shall not make any cuttings in your flesh for the dead, nor print any marks upon you; I am the Lord." In ancient days, these practices were done to appease the god of death and the grave. They were associated with sorcery and witchcraft (see the same biblical context-Leviticus 19:31). In many pagan cultures today, this is associated with demonic practices such as sorcery and witchcraft.

It is not by accident we are now witnessing an alarming and fast-growing trend of bizarre body piercing and tattoos in America. These are external symbols of a demonic society!

Furthermore, these demons had forced their victim out of society, away from family and friends to live in isolation in the tombs of the dead. Notice also that after he was set free, he did not want to live in isolation. Instead, he wanted to be with Jesus and His disciples (see Luke 8:38). But Jesus commanded him to be a witness to his own people. The Bible reports, "And he went his way, and published throughout the whole city how great things Jesus had done unto him" (Luke 8:39).

All cults and false religions isolate their followers from all outside influences. The aim is to brainwash their victims and indoctrinate them with lies. The cults and false religions want to manipulate and control their victims. This is the satanic method of isolation and indoctrination. In our text, the demons had isolated this man from his family and friends for a reason. They wanted to exert greater control of him for the kingdom of darkness.

God has created mankind in His own image. He said, "Let us make man in our image, after our likeness …" (Genesis 1:26). The one and only triune God of three persons has known and enjoyed intimate fellowship within the Trinity for all of eternity. The fact we have been created in His image means many things, including that we have been created as social creatures. We have been created to have fellowship with God and with each other. We all need family and friends. The Bible is filled with many admonitions that remind us of the wisdom that is found in the counsel of those around us. When isolated to ourselves, we can be vulnerable to pride, deception, depression, and foolishness.

Our world is now at a very unusual and exceptional time in history that has created a social climate of isolation. It is strange that we live during the time of the world's greatest population. The world's population is now more than 7.6 billion and growing at the rate of 1.5 million per week! At the same time, in most cultures people are less social and less interactive with their family and friends than ever before! What has contributed to this development?

Our very lifestyles in the last few decades have promoted personal independence and isolation. Our entertainment and technological toys have created a constant temptation to selfishly immerse our whole being into a world that embraces the philosophies and pleasures being espoused by people that we do not know on a personal level. People spend countless hours glued to a television set, surfing the Internet or playing mindless computer games. Some even wear headphones and bombard their minds with illicit musical lyrics. As a result, people have forgotten how to relate to each other. Family members who live in the same house are so mentally isolated from one another they are virtual strangers. Any attempt to pull people away from their toys or entertainment brings anger or boredom. This is because they are self-centered and are only interesting in their own agendas. People do not know how to love sacrificially. They have no desire to make themselves open to the counsel and help from others.

In addition to this, our affluence has also made us even more vulnerable to independence and isolation. Just a few decades ago we lived in a community where people were all dependent upon each other. The people who taught their kids were their friends. The man at the grocery store was their neighbor, or at least a friend of a friend. Everyone took time to visit with their family and friends. When there was a need, people in the community knew about it and got involved. But we now live in a society where most people do not even know the names of their neighbors. More shocking, there are many things within their own family that we do not know. What has happened?

Families in the past spent a lot of time together. They worked together. They traveled together. They ate meals together. They made it a point to go to church together and attend social gatherings. Furthermore, they prayed together. They read the Bible together. They laughed and wept together. Needless to say, we are living in a culture where our time-saving devices are not giving us more time to spend with God or each other. We are living in an age where we have more to do than ever before. We are being hurried at a frantic pace. We must ask, "Where are we going?"

Satan is smiling! Our thirst for materialism, pleasure, and power has led us to become growingly independent and isolated. As a result, an overwhelming majority of people in our culture have become extremely self-centered. Listen to this warning, "This know also, that in the last days perilous times shall come. For men shall be lovers of their own selves, covetous, boasters, proud, blasphemers, disobedient to parents, unthankful, unholy, without natural affection, trucebreakers, false accusers, incontinent, fierce, despisers of those that are good, traitors, heady, [high-minded], lovers of pleasures more than lovers of God; having a form of godliness, but denying the power thereof: from such turn away" (2 Timothy 3:1-5). Our society is a perfect reflection of this prophecy, and the marks of a demonic society are becoming more prevalent as we become even more independent and isolated from each other, and especially from our Lord!

Observation #4 about the nature of a demonic society: The final achievement in the move toward a demonic society is the attempt to remove the power and presence of the God of the Bible from that culture (Luke 8:36-37).

Notice that after the people in this man's community saw he had been set free and had been changed, they did not rejoice. Instead, they were filled with another fear. They had witnessed the power and presence of God, and they demanded Jesus leave them alone (Luke 8:37).

In essence, they were more afraid of the Son of God than they were of the demons living among them. This is always the final step of divine judgment (see Romans 1:18-28). This was a society that "did not like to retain God in their knowledge" (Romans 1:28). Isn't it ironic that many in America are more afraid of born-again evangelical Christians than they are of radical Muslims who promote jihad around the world?

People have been rejecting God since the beginning of time! Godly people have been killed and persecuted by the ungodly throughout the course of human history! However, our world has witnessed more believers in Jesus Christ who have been killed in the last century than in the previous 19 centuries combined! The demons are leading the world on a frenzy to stop tolerating the spiritual light. Demons want to extinguish God's light! Demons fear the light because it exposes them. It is only a matter of time before the demons will make this final move in our society. Can you think of a powerful religion that is spreading around the world? Isn't it odd that this religion promotes brutal violence and its adherents dream of a heaven where sexual orgies are the reward for killing innocent people, especially Jews and Christians?

America is unwittingly leading the world down the path toward this demonic society. Consider the fact that the U.S. is the world leader in rock music. It is my opinion that the loud driving music and wicked lyrics of rock music is one of Satan's primary tools to destroy the minds and capture the souls of our youth. They are being enslaved to his kingdom of darkness. Travel the world and you will hear this music and you will witness the demonic culture it is helping to create. America is the world's primary exporter of pornography, entertainment, and technology. America is also helping the world worship the god of materialism.

We are creating a new generation that is under the influence of demons! This generation will become demon possessed. Get ready, America! The demonic culture you are promoting as freedom of speech has enslaved the minds and souls of our sons and daughters. We are paying a horrible price and we will pay an even more horrific price! God, have mercy on us!

CHAPTER 12

America and the Spiritual Point of No Return

"My spirit shall not always strive with man."
Genesis 6:3

IF AMERICA AND OUR WORLD HAVE NOT REACHED THE spiritual point of no return, they are getting perilously close. The Spirit of God has reminded me America is spiritually where Israel was in the days of the prophet Isaiah. Please read Isaiah 1:2- 9. The only reason God had not yet judged Israel was because of a godly remnant. Like Israel of old, I personally believe this is the only reason the Lord has not yet crushed the United States in judgment. Will He wait until after the Rapture to severely judge America? We do not know. He is sovereign.

According to the Bible, a person, a city, a church, a nation, and a culture can spiritually reach the point of no return. They reach this tragic moment when they have silenced their conscience. This means the Lord's work of grace and restraint from evil in their lives ceases to exist. Consequently, they are left to their own foolish and ultimate demise. When these people reach this point, they cannot be saved and are ripe for the ultimate judgment of God.

The cultural symptoms that are always prevalent when a society has reached the spiritual point of no return have rapidly intensified since the early 1960s. This can be concluded from the following biblical case studies. The Lord directed His prophets and apostles to give His people at least four historical examples of societies that reached the spiritual point of no return. Each of these cultures was severely crushed by His divine judgment. They were: (1) The days of Noah- Genesis 6-7; (2) The cities of Sodom and Gomorrah- Genesis 18-19; (3) The Canaanite societies that were cast out by Israel- Genesis 15:13-16; Leviticus 18:1-30; 20:1-27; Deuteronomy 18:9-14; 1 Kings 14:24; and (4) The historical degeneration of Old Testament Israel- 1 Kings 14:24; Isaiah 1:1-9; 3:9-26; 4:20; 8:19-22.

What took place in each of these societies should be compared to the divine commentary found in Romans 1:18-32. The cultural symptoms mentioned in Scripture speak of the global societies that will reach the point of no return in the last days (Daniel 8:23; 1Timothy 4:1-3; 2 Timothy 3:1-9; Revelation 9:20-21).

These biblical passages help us develop a clear picture of the cultural symptoms that are always displayed in a society that has reached the spiritual point of no return. Two things always happen in a society that has no conscience. There will be no private or public restraint of evil, and demonic influence and possession will escalate. Each of these will be visibly manifested.

When the conscience, God's spiritual warning system, has been turned off in a person or culture, it will be void of any fear of God or man. In such a society there will only be one authority – self! The apostle Paul described this when he said, "This know also, that in the last days perilous [dangerous, terrible] times shall come. For men shall be lovers of their own selves..." (2 Timothy 3:1-2). In the following verses of this passage, he described the wicked people and their hideous sins that we read about in our daily newspapers and hear about on the evening news.

In a society that has reached the spiritual point of no return there will be no remorse or shame on the part of those who commit public acts of brutal violence and murder – there will be no respect for human life. Evil people will engage in acts of sexually deviant behavior and flaunt a lifestyle with no moral restraint. Many people will defy all the laws of God and man while exhibiting a spirit of rebellion and lawlessness. Their speech will become vulgar and indecent. Their vocabulary will be filled with cursing and blasphemous remarks and gestures. Their language will be crude, lewd, and downright filthy. People's lifestyles will be filled with deceit, envy, and greed. They will become wicked gluttons, living to gratify their senses. Life will be riveted upon the pleasure of self.

In essence, the conscience-free society will have no moral boundaries. A philosophy of cultural relativism [when the end justifies the means] will permeate society. Such a lifestyle will center on personal freedom to pursue the passions of depravity. People will not want "to retain God in their knowledge" (Romans 1:28). Their hatred for God, His Word, His people, and anything that promotes His laws will become prominent (Romans 1:29-31). The righteous saints will watch their standing in society move from one of toleration to persecution. Finally, believers will become subject to aggressive and malicious martyrdom (John 15:18-27; Revelation 6:9-11).

When this society has reached the spiritual point of no return, two sins become prevalent: homosexuality (Genesis 18-19; Leviticus 18:22-25; 1 Kings 14:24; Romans 1:26), and occultism [sorcery, witchcraft, black magic, divination, and astrology] (Deuteronomy 18:9-14; Isaiah 8:19-22; Revelation 9:21). These two sins seem to always display open and defiant rebellion against God.

When a culture is sensitive to their God-given conscience, they are being influenced by the gracious work of the Holy Spirit. However, when people suppress the revelation of God in their conscience (see Romans 1:18-19), it opens the way for increased demonic influence and possession.

Demons are described as "unclean spirits" forty-six times in the Bible. Jesus used this descriptive label for demons many times. This designates them as being immoral, filthy, wicked, and vile in their nature, just like their master – Satan. The early church equated a sensual spirit with demonic influence (James 3:15). Demons play on the sensual desires of human beings. They appeal to their sensual appetites in ways that do not honor God. Demons always seek to inflict destruction to the soul, body, mind, and conscience of their victims. Demons love to captivate human minds and bodies to gratify their wicked desires and wreck the lives of those who have been created in the image of God. Most Bible scholars believe this played a major role in the divine condemnation that brought about the destruction of the world in Noah's day (Genesis 6:1-13).

The very core nature of Satan and his demons is death, destruction, and damnation (John 8:44; 10:10; Revelation 9:11). They love to torment people and abuse them both mentally and physically. Demons can influence people to commit acts of great violence with the use of superhuman strength. They can cause an individual to display nudity with no shame. People under demonic influence commonly exhibit weird and abnormal behavior. And very often they abuse the body of their victims, sometimes in the absence of pain. (In the gospels, all of this was displayed in the life of one man – Matthew 8:28; Mark 5:1-5; Luke 8:26-29).

It is my personal opinion that demonic influence is on the rise in all levels of our society. Look at the cuttings and tattoos people are inflicting on their bodies. Drug use is escalating and there is a growing fascination with vampires, scorpions, snakes, spiders, and skulls. Historically, these are all external manifestations of demonic influence.

When the collective conscience of a society is "seared," people will begin to cling to "seducing spirits and doctrines of demons." (1 Timothy 4:1-2) At the heart of the doctrine of demons is the ultimate lie – the inversion of reality. Isaiah sounded the warning of this doctrine long ago, "Woe to them that call evil good, and good evil; that put darkness for light, and light for darkness; that put bitter for sweet, and sweet for bitter" (Isaiah 5:20).

Demonic cultures move their subjects from good to evil. Under this influence, people move from moral purity to deviant immoral behavior. The godly culture of love is transformed into a culture filled with hate. The culture of peace is lured into expressions of violence. In a culture that obeys God's law, people restraint their passions. But in the demonic culture people defiantly flaunt their passions, displaying lawlessness.

The godly culture celebrates life while the demonic culture celebrates death. Most tragic of all, Satan completely blinds their eyes to invert reality – God becomes Satan, and Satan becomes God.

When a culture reaches the point of no return, they will commit evil acts and think of them as deeds of obedience and worship to their god. Murder, adultery, deceit, and hate are all justified in their inverted value system because their conscience is dead and their mind is being driven by demons and their wicked doctrine. Jesus warned His disciples the day would come when "whosoever killeth you will think that he doeth God service" (John 16:2). Once again, I want to ask you: Can you think of any religion in the world that celebrates violence, deceit, and hatred toward the people of God? Can you think of a religion that describes its heaven as a place of sexual orgy? The fact that Islam is the fastest growing religion in the world is a powerful testimony that our world is marching toward the point of no return at an incredible speed. Please remember what Revelation 21:8 says, "But the fearful, and unbelieving, and the abominable, and murderers, and whoremongers, and sorcerers, and idolaters, and all liars, shall have their part in the lake which burneth with fire and brimstone: which is the second death."

Satan's great motive in blinding the mind and destroying the conscience of man is to damn his soul. The apostle Paul revealed this when he wrote, "…the god of this world hath blinded the minds of them which believe not, lest the light of the glorious gospel of Christ, who is the image of God, should shine unto them" (2 Corinthians 4:4).

If you are playing with sin and trying to silence God's warning in your conscience, please stop and think about what you are doing. You are spiritually moving down a path of degeneration that at some point will take control of you, and you will be damned forever! Only Jesus can set you free from the power and guilt of all your sin! "If the Son therefore shall make you free, ye shall be free indeed" (John 8:36). Only the shed blood of Jesus, God's lamb, can "purge your conscience from dead works to serve the living God" (Hebrews 9:14).

Our world is running out of time. How long will God wait before His great wrath falls from heaven upon this wicked generation? The answer to that question lies in the biblical historical pattern of God's judgment of nations or societies when they reached the ultimate spiritual point of no return.

The scoffers in the first century were taunting the church with the question, "Where is the promise of his coming?" (2 Peter 3:4) Peter's response pointed to the patience of our gracious Lord because He "was not willing that any should perish, but that all should come to repentance."

Let us examine God's track record of how long He has been willing to wait for a culture to be saturated with the spiritual point of no return before He visits them with awesome acts of His vengeance. Remember that the Lord has promised, "Vengeance is mine: I will repay" (Romans 12:19).

The Days of Noah: In the days of Noah, God waited until "the wickedness of man was great in the earth, and that every imagination of the thoughts of his heart was only evil continually. ... and the earth was filled with violence. ... for all flesh had corrupted his way upon the earth" (Genesis 6:5, 12- 13). With the exception of eight people, the wickedness of Noah's generation permeated the entire global population. People constantly dwelt on wickedness in their thoughts and action. Think about how long God waited!

The Canaanite Societies: In Genesis 15:13-16, God told Abraham his descendants would have to wait four generations before they could displace the inhabitants of the land of Canaan because "the iniquity of the Amorites was not yet full" (Genesis 15:16). Over 600 years actually passed (from the time of this announcement to Abram until the conquest under Joshua) before God was willing to command the Jewish people to destroy all the inhabitants of the Promised Land. The Lord, according to His great patience and grace, waited until their sin was "full" – the spiritual point of no return had completely saturated the culture. The archeological remains they are uncovering in Israel from this period of time confirm that the Canaanite culture was filled with gross immoralities and brutal violence. The culture was in a mode of self-destruction. Think about how long God waited!

The Wickedness of Sodom: When God destroyed the cities of Sodom and Gomorrah it was because the sin of homosexuality was "very grievous" to Him (Genesis 18:20). This sin had totally saturated these two cities. In Genesis 19:4 the homosexual crowd that gathered around the house of Lot demanded the release of the two visiting men (really angels sent from God) to them so that they could sexually abuse them all night. This crowd was described as "both old and young, all the people from every quarter" (Genesis 19:4). Remember the Lord had promised Abraham if there were ten righteous people in these cities he would not destroy them (Genesis 18:32). Only four people escaped the sudden divine judgment upon these two wicked cities. However, Lot's wife disobeyed the Lord and looked back and was turned into a pillar of salt (Genesis 19:26). In the days following, Lot's daughters made him drunk and they had an incestuous relationship with their father and gave birth to two boys. The boys became the fathers of the Moabites and the Ammonites (Genesis 19:30-38). (Recent archeological evidence confirms the biblical record concerning the destruction of Sodom and Gomorrah. The remains of these cities are located on the Jordanian side of the southern end of the Dead Sea.) Think about how long God waited!

Old Testament Israel's Divine Judgment: When Israel came into the land, the Lord told them to destroy all the wicked inhabitants and warned if they did not, they would be polluted with their sins, and they would worship their gods (Deuteronomy 7:1-5). Israel did not obey and eventually followed the sinful path of the wicked Canaanites. God waited 700 of years before He brought in the Assyrians to ruthlessly carry away the northern ten tribes of Israel into exile in 722 B.C. Finally, He waited an additional 136 years, until 586 B.C., before He brought vengeance upon the remaining Jewish people in the land. He used the brutal Babylonians to kill most of the Jewish population of the two southern tribes, destroy Jerusalem, plunder the temple, and carry away a remnant into Babylon. Once again, the Lord exercised great patience and mercy until each group's culture was saturated with symptoms of the spiritual point on no return. In the days of King Rehoboam, almost 350 years before the Babylonian destruction of Judah, the Bible records what the culture of Judah was like, "And there were sodomites in the land: and they did according to all the abominations of the nations which the LORD cast out before the children of Israel" (1 Kings 14:24). Think about how long God waited!

The Last Days' Divine Global Judgment: The historical cases above cast a clear shadow of God's divine patience into the future. According to Daniel 8:23, the Antichrist will come to power when "the transgressors are come to the <u>full</u>" (Daniel 8:23). This statement is similar to the one God made to Abraham in Genesis 15:16 about waiting for His judgment because "the iniquity of the Amorites is not yet <u>full</u>." This would indicate the Lord will once again wait until the cultural symptoms that display the point of no return have totally permeated the nations at the end of time.

Does this mean that the Lord will not come until the majority of the world's population has adopted or applauds homosexuality and occultism? Not necessarily!

Because the events of the last days will eventually usher in the Kingdom of God, the judgment of God will be a little different. The Lord has revealed with amazing detail the events of the last days.

The Lord has determined that He has a unique way for His bride, the church, to exit this world. This is why it is called a "mystery" in 1 Corinthians 15:51. According to the Scriptures, the global professing church will experience a time of spiritual collapse when the end comes (2 Thessalonians 2:3; 1Timothy 4:1-3; 2 Timothy 4:1-4). This was also portrayed by the church of Laodicea (Revelation 3:14-22). Therefore, the professing church will conclude its divine mission earth as a weak restraining influence. Finally, at this moment of weakness, the true church will be supernaturally removed from the earth in the Rapture, before the tribulation begins. Thus, the unique ministry of the Holy Spirit's indwelling of the true believer will come to an end. This will be the removal of the unique restraining influence of the Holy Spirit through the church that will take place at the Rapture (2 Thessalonians 2:6-7).

After the apostle Paul spoke of the removal of the restraining influence of the Holy Spirit through the church he wrote, "And then shall that Wicked [Lawless One] be revealed..." (2 Thessalonians 2:8). The context demands this is a reference to the Antichrist. Therefore, we must conclude the Antichrist cannot officially step onto the stage of human history until the true church has been removed. When he comes on the scene, he will be unrestrained in his promotion and portrayal of wickedness and lawlessness during the Tribulation. It will be during this period of time that the world will travel down the final steps of the path to the point of no return.

Think about this! The work of the Holy Spirit to restrain the world from evil by the presence of the church will suddenly disappear as the church supernaturally exits the earth. This will also take place at a moment in history when the overwhelming majority of the population that is left behind will, in essence, not possess a functioning conscience. Many of them will have previously reached the point of no return so that the Holy Spirit will no longer be able to restrain them in their conscience. This will open the way for the entrance of the Antichrist and his hellish kingdom of darkness to take over the world.

The days of the tribulation will be totally unique (Matthew 24:21-22). It will be a time of incredible wickedness, immorality, violence, and deception. Human governments will totally discard the Word of God and unite in their global campaign against the Lord (Psalm 2:1-3). The collective unrestrained global culture will act like brute beasts. The laws of decency and respect for human life will be totally abandoned. The lowest forms of decadence, debasement, deception, and disrespect for God and man will become the norm.

The Lord will graciously send the final tribulation generation many witnesses who will warn the world and proclaim the gospel of Jesus

Christ. He will send them two Jewish witnesses, accompanied by the display of incredible supernatural powers (Revelation 11:1-6). These two great men of God will no doubt have a major influence in the salvation, divine anointing, and training of 144,000 young Jewish men, who will be called out of the twelve tribes of Israel and sent to the nations of the world as evangelists proclaiming the gospel of Jesus Christ (Revelation 7:1-8; 14:1-5).

Furthermore, in Israel, the Lord will raise up a large group of Jewish witnesses who will "keep the commandments of God, and have the testimony of Jesus Christ" (Revelation 12:17). These believers will be uniquely empowered by the Holy Spirit, and will be entrusted with a divine ministry of deliverance that will be centered "in Mount Zion and in Jerusalem" (Joel 2:28-32). All of this will be accompanied by the ongoing wrathful judgment of God that will be recognized as being divine in origin (Revelation 6:15-18).

Even after all this occurs, an overwhelming majority of the masses on earth will violently reject the gospel and continue in their demonic state. Concerning these people, the apostle John wrote, "And the rest of the men which were not killed by these plagues yet repented not of the works of their hands, that they should not worship [demons], … Neither repented they of their murders, nor of their sorceries, nor of their fornication, nor of their thefts" (Revelation 9:20-21).

We live in a culture that is flirting with the ultimate point of no return! America is experiencing the symptoms of a culture that has reached its deadly termination. It has not yet permeated the entire society, but that minority has become extremely militant. All the while, there does not seem to be much of an effort to stand against the tide of filth that is drowning America. In my opinion, the senior saints are in most cases the bulk of the divine salt that is preserving the U.S. Should our Lord's coming for His church occur in another couple of decades, we cannot begin to imagine the impact this would have on our culture. When most of these senior saints pass into the presence of our Lord, the absence of their spiritual influence as "the salt of the earth" (Matthew 5:13) will have a major impact on the acceleration of our world's race toward the spiritual point of no return. Our society is becoming more pagan, sensual, and demonic with each passing day! America is inverting reality! The pace of this inversion is accelerating at an enormous rate!

As this occurs around us, I find it most disturbing to observe that the church has become a part of the problem. Instead of warning the world and being a part of the solution, the church seems to be focused upon identifying with the pagan culture. The professing church is focused upon pleasing sinful people in the culture rather than pleasing our holy God in heaven. They have traded the approval of God for the applause of men. It seems very few believers are hungering and thirsting after righteousness. The professing church has "a form of godliness, but [denies] the power thereof …." (2 Timothy 3:5). The Biblical admonition is: "…from such turn away" (2 Timothy 3:5).

Those who are being led by the Spirit of God will be in tune with His will and they will understand what is about to take place in our world. These dear servants of God will faithfully sound out the warning that our world is rapidly reaching the spiritual point of no return and the age of grace is about to end.

God has always called His faithful and courageous servants to mercifully and compassionately warn their generation to flee from His wrath to come. I want to be one of these servants of God. How about you?

CHAPTER 13

My Prayer: May God Have Mercy on America

"If my people, which are called by my name, shall
humble themselves, and pray, and seek my face,
and turn from their wicked ways; then will I hear from
heaven, and will forgive their sin, and will heal their land."
2 Chronicles 7:14

MAY THE LORD GOD HAVE MERCY UPON THE UNITED
States of America. That is the cry of my heart as I am burdened
to pray for my country and as I witness its moral and spiritual decline.
I sense in my soul that our nation is about to suffer from a major act(s)
of divine judgment. No one can pretend to know what this act of divine
judgment will be or when it will occur – but it is coming!

As I witness my country ever increasingly turn its back on God, I
am reminded of the great Jewish prophet, Elijah. Elijah marched into the
throne room of wicked King Ahab one day and announced that divine
judgment in the form of a drought was about to fall upon Israel (1 Kings
17:1). Where did he get such a revelation that this was about to happen?
Elijah walked with God. He knew God had warned the Jewish nation
that if they ever departed from Him and disobeyed His Word, He would
curse them and send a drought as an act of judgment (Deuteronomy
28:23-24). Elijah saw the spiritual and moral corruption of his people.

He knew their sin had reached a point where it was time for God to keep His Word and judge His people. In other words, Elijah was taking God at His Word. In his soul, he sensed the time of God's retribution with a drought was imminent. Elijah cared more about the glory of God than he did about the prosperity of his own nation.

Similarly, as I look around America and witness the great spiritual and moral corruption, I sense in my soul that the time of God's divine judgment upon our nation is growing more imminent. God will honor His Word! I am not a prophet, and like all believers today, I can never pretend to know the exact timing or nature of God's divine judgment.

At this very hour, America continues to exhibit a haughty spirit of rebellion against God and His Word. There is a hunger for the sinful pleasures of every sexual perversion that is an abomination to our Holy God. A lifestyle of violence, lawlessness, and deception permeates the land. Many Americans have turned from the One and only living God and are flocking to various religious expressions of paganism. Too many Americans are fascinated with witchcraft, sorcery, mind-altering drugs, and other bizarre activities that are an offense to the Lord. An ever-growing spirit of greed, accompanied by a relentless pursuit of the idols of money and power, has a spiritual death-grip on the nation. The God-ordained order of marriage and the home is disintegrating right before our eyes. Our nation is spiritually adrift, morally bankrupt, and politically divided. It appears the United States stands on the brink of economic collapse and political upheaval.

However, the greatest problem in America is the godless condition of the majority of local churches. The spiritual and moral collapse of America is a commentary on the failure of the church to be salt and light to the world (Matthew 5:13-16). The professing church has become a part of the problem, rather than a part of the solution in America! A majority of pastors and church leaders have turned our churches into nothing more than social clubs. In these churches people dwell on religious platitudes, and even condone or promote godlessness within their congregation. There is very little talk about sin, repentance, the holiness of God, divine judgment, or eternal punishment. It seems the leadership of American church is driving home a false message that we can convince God to bless us so we can be happy now. Little is said in churches today about heaven or eternity. In essence, the church has become like the world. Professing Christians thrive on instant gratification. It is all about the god of self. God gets relegated to some lesser position of importance in our daily lives when He should be number one.

While reflecting upon all of this, the Spirit of God directed my attention to Daniel 9:1-19. In this great passage, the godly prophet of Israel, Daniel, had discovered that his people were about to be released from their captivity of almost seventy years in Babylon. Being the godly man that he was, Daniel immediately began to wonder if this would be the time when the temple would be rebuilt in Jerusalem. In light of the response of the angel Gabriel to his prayer, it appears Daniel wondered if this was the time the Messiah and His kingdom would arrive.

While Daniel contemplated the coming of the Messiah and His temple, he realized his people were not spiritually ready for their long-promised Messiah. Consequently, he began to confess his sin to the Lord, as well as the sin of his people – Israel (Daniel 9:3-20).

For a number of years, I have been deeply moved every time I read the prayer of this godly prophet. Daniel had a deep and abiding love for his God and his people. He was broken over the spiritual condition of his people and realized they were not ready for the opportunity to rebuild the holy temple in Jerusalem and welcome and worship the Messiah.

Please understand my heart. I am not even remotely suggesting I should be compared to this godly prophet of God. I am, at best, a spiritual pigmy when compared to Daniel. However, I share his brokenness over the condition of my nation. I, too, have a deep love for my God and a sense the church of America is not ready for the Rapture. And, those who will be caught up to heaven are not really contemplating the reality that they will soon stand in the presence of the holy Lord Jesus and give an account of their lives since the day of their salvation (2 Corinthians 5:10).

Should our Lord not come in the next few years, it is highly likely that every Christian in this country is going to suffer the consequences of living in a nation that has turned its back on God. Only those whose lives are deeply anchored in the Word of God and walking in His Spirit will be able to glorify our Lord and rejoice in the midst of the suffering that will come.

The Lord has directed me to write out a prayer of confession and repentance for America in the final chapter of this book. I am seeking the guidance of the Holy Spirit through the Word of God to help guide our thinking and praying to provoke us all to get on our knees and cry out to God for mercy on behalf of America. I will include in this written prayer certain biblical passages that you should read to guide you in this effort.

Before I begin with this written prayer, I must share with you an experience I had which I consider not to be a coincidence. These kinds of things happen to me all the time while I am thinking about preaching or writing about God's Word. While I was driving to a speaking engagement a few years ago, I stopped at a rest area. As I walked back to my van, my attention was drawn to a photo-copied page that was on the dashboard of the passenger side of a car parked beside of me. Before this stop, the Lord had been speaking to my heart about writing out this prayer and I was wrestling with this assignment in my mind. I had never done anything like this before. However, when I saw this paper on the dashboard, I knew the Lord was dealing with me about this assignment. The topic of the copied page, turned perfectly so I could read it without turning my head, was: "Abraham's Intercession on Behalf of Wicked Sodom." As I got in my van and drove away, my mind went back to Genesis 18 and the account of Abraham's pleading with God to not destroy Sodom and Gomorrah. I believe there is a reason why the Spirit of God chose to give us this great chapter in the Bible. It is a testimony to how the godly must cry out to the Lord for mercy when it is evident divine judgment is about to fall upon their society. As I drove further down the interstate, my mind was flooded with what the Lord wanted me to write in this prayer. I could hardly drive for the tears that streamed down my face.

I plead with you to take this seriously. We must seek the face of God in this matter. I am not motivated to do this because I am a great patriot of America, though I am. However, I am motivated to do this because there are still millions of Americans that need to hear the gospel and be saved. I am motivated to do this because I want my God to be glorified in spite of all of this wickedness, deception, and confusion in America. I hunger to see a real revival among a remnant of godly people and churches! I must also confess I need to pray this because I have some family members who are not walking with the Lord. I deeply care about them and what lies ahead in the future.

As you read this prayer, I sincerely hope you will join me on my knees in brokenness and confession before our God for our own sins and for the sins of America. I also appeal to you to share copies of this book with other believers so they can join us in praying for our nation at this vital hour. Perhaps you could make this a prayerful time for your discipleship group or Bible class at your church.

Join me in this prayer.

Oh Holy Father in heaven, we come to You in the Name of Your Son, Jesus Christ. We desire to pray in the power of the Holy Spirit. We humbly come into Your divine presence with a sense of awe and reverence. We come before You in a spirit of worship, praise, and thanksgiving. We thank You for the gift of Your eternal Son, the Lord Jesus Christ. We acknowledge You as the One and only triune God, revealed in three persons who are equally God – Father, Son, and Holy Spirit (Genesis 1:26 and Matthew 28:19).

We thank You for loving us and sending Your Son to die for our sins (John 3:16 and Romans 5:8-11). We thank You for the gift of eternal life through His personal sacrifice on the cross (Romans 6:23 and 1 Corinthians 15:1-3), and His physical resurrection from the dead (1 Corinthians 15:4-19). We thank You for the promise we have that He will soon return to take us to live with Him in heaven (John 14:3; Acts 1:11; and 1 Thessalonians 4:13-18). "Even so, come, Lord Jesus" (Revelation 22:20).

Oh Lord, we believe that Your Son, according to Your revelation, created the heavens and the earth, "and all that in them is" (Exodus 20:11) in six days and rested on the seventh day. We believe He created the world out of nothing (Hebrews 11:3). Nothing is impossible with You (Luke 1:37). You have all power and authority upon this earth and in all of creation (Matthew 28:18).

You are holy, righteous, and just. You can do no wrong and You have never sinned or acted in an evil way. Everything You have ever done, or will do, is good. You are a good, gracious, kind, and merciful God.

All of us who have lived on this earth have sinned against You. "For all have sinned, and come short of the glory of God" (Romans 3:23). Not one of us can say we are righteous or good (Romans 3:10). At our spiritual core, our souls, we are "deceitful above all things, and desperately wicked" (Jeremiah 17:9). None of us, without the work of Your Spirit, are seeking to know You or follow You (Romans 3:11-12). "All we like sheep have gone astray; we have turned everyone to his own way" (Isaiah 53:6).

Oh Lord, forgive us! We do not want to wander from Your presence. We want to abide in Your presence by the sweet work of Your Holy Spirit (John 15:1-11). We acknowledge that without the work of the Holy Spirit we cannot know You or understand the things of God (1 Corinthians 2:9-16). With His help, we want to "trust in the LORD with all of [our] heart; and lean not unto [our] own understanding" (Proverbs 3:5). We want to acknowledge Your presence in all that we do (Proverbs 3:6).

Oh Lord, we come to You on behalf of our nation, America. We thank You that Your hand has been upon this nation for many years. You have blessed this nation. In Your Word, You have declared: "Blessed is the nation whose God is the LORD" (Psalm 33:12).

We know this nation as a whole has never been a godly nation. However, we know that from its inception there was a godly remnant that settled this land and established a government that respected, honored, and reflected the Word of God. It has been an honor to live in a land where its people have been free to worship You. We rejoice that we have been able to openly and freely proclaim the gospel of Jesus Christ. We thank You that for hundreds of years, Your church has been able to saturate this land with the preaching and teaching of the Word of God. We are grateful we have been able to send out missionaries to the nations of the world to proclaim the gospel of Jesus Christ, and the salvation that comes only in His name (Acts 4:12).

We acknowledge that You are sovereign over all nations (Romans 13:1). All of the nations are nothing when compared to You (Isaiah 40:15 -23). Global history from the creation to the end is in Your hands. You are the One who establishes the nations, selects kings, and removes them (Daniel 2:21). We believe that You have chosen this nation as a special instrument in Your hand for the good and freedom of many nations. It has been Your desire that this nation would give protection to Your people, both Jews and Christians. It is very apparent this nation has played a significant role in the establishment, recognition, and protection of the nation of Israel in the last century.

Oh Lord, as we look at America today through the holy eyes of Your Word. Our hearts are broken. It is apparent the attitude of respect and honor for You as the One and only God is rapidly departing from America. O Lord, we believe the first of the great Ten Commandments that You gave to Israel is still the first commandment from heaven for all mankind, "Thou shalt have no other gods before me" (Exodus 20:3). We know America is grieving Your heart as they follow after other idols and gods that do not exist. Oh God, have mercy upon America!

Oh Lord, forgive us for the spirit of rebellion and haughty defiance against Your holiness and Your holy standards written in the Word of God. May there be a spirit of shame, conviction, and brokenness that would break out in this land, bringing some to repentance. We grieve to know our government, media, entertainment industry, and education centers are promoting a lifestyle of sexual immorality throughout the land. We know that such an open acceptance of these kinds of sins are an abomination in Your sight and historically have invited Your divine judgment (Leviticus 18:19-29). Oh God, have mercy upon America!

Oh Lord, we live in a land of murderers. We are killing our unborn children for the sake of convenience and selfish ambitions. We are no different from the pagan cultures of ancient history that offered their babies to their gods, while living lives of gross immorality (Deuteronomy 18:10). Every day Americans are being killed by others who are filled with hate, wickedness, and murder. Oh God, have mercy upon America!

Oh Lord, we live in a land of gross demonic deception. Our culture is obsessed with witchcraft, sorcery, astrology, and many other forms of demonic pagan practices and expressions (Deuteronomy 18:9-14). Our children are constantly playing games that saturate their minds with evil, violence, demons, murder, pornography, and many other sexual perversions. We know You have said that a person becomes what they think about (Proverbs 22:6). Oh Lord, we are already reaping the consequences of all of this ungodly and wicked entertainment. We fear for the future of our nation. We know demons are taking control of the minds of many of our children, while parents are obsessed with gratifying themselves with pleasures and materialism. Oh God, have mercy upon America!

Oh Lord, we live in a nation where governmental leaders and educators are promoting rebellion against You, the destruction of marriage and the home, the destruction of our nation, and the damnation of our people. They are giving freedoms and privileges to Muslims while restricting these same freedoms and privileges to Christians in every level of our society. Oh Lord, the prophecy of Psalm 2:1-3 is coming to pass in America. Oh God, have mercy upon America!

Oh Lord, the greatest sin in America is within the professing churches of America. The spiritual condition of America is a reflection of the failure of the church in America to proclaim and live Your holy standards [like the prophets in Jeremiah's day (Jeremiah 23:16-32)]. The pastors and people of the churches have sinned against You. Our churches are filled with sin. The lives of professing Christians in most cases are no different than those who make no claim of being a Christian. Most church members do not really want to hear the truth and be convicted about their sins. They have hired pastors who will entertain them and make them feel good about themselves (2 Timothy 4:3-4). Most professing Christians seldom read their Bibles and rarely weep over their sins or confess them to You. The churches of America are filled with sinners who do not know You. Those on the outside of the church see this hypocrisy and have no respect for the church or the Bible. Oh God, raise up godly men who will exhibit the spirit of Elijah and take a bold stand for their Lord. Oh God, send a revival among the saved pastors that have allowed sin to keep them from having fellowship with You. May they repent and boldly proclaim the Word of God. May they provide their congregations with godly leadership in these days of spiritual apostasy and deception. May they not compromise Your truth. May they not be afraid of anyone but You! May they allow the Spirit of God to work through them to "reprove the word of sin, and of righteousness, and of judgment" (John 16:8).

Oh Lord, the church needs to awaken from its spiritual sleep and proclaim that the triune God of the Bible is the One and only God. We know that in this present society a false message of tolerance is being proclaimed. However, those who call for tolerance are intolerant when it comes to the exclusive worship of You, the God of the Bible. The church must lovingly and firmly take a stand on this truth. The message of the Bible is clear. Jesus Christ, and the gospel message that is anchored in His life, death, and resurrection, is the one and only message of salvation (John 14:6; Acts 4:12; and 1 Timothy 2:5). We have been exhorted to pray for the salvation of others because You "will have all men to be saved, and to come unto the knowledge of the truth" (1 Timothy 2:4). You are "not willing that any should perish, but that all should come to repentance" (2 Peter 3:9). Oh God, have mercy on the pastors and people in our churches in America!

Oh Lord, we deserve Your divine judgment at this very hour! We are grieving You! This nation has turned from its biblical foundation and is promoting evil, lawlessness, and rebellion in our homes, communities, public schools, universities, and churches. I fear we have gone too far. I fear we are about to cross the spiritual point of no return. Oh Lord, I am crying out to You for mercy on behalf of my country. I do this because of the example of godly Abraham when he interceded for wicked Sodom (Genesis 18:16-33). Oh Lord, I am praying this because Moses did this for his people. (Exodus 32:7-14) This was the heart of the great prophet

Elijah, when he took that bold stand on Mount Carmel and prayed for a display of Your power to turn the heart of his people back to You (1 Kings 18:21-40). This was the burden of Daniel and of all of the prophets of the Old Testament as You moved them to write to their people to warn them of Your divine judgment because of their sin. This was also the heart of the messages of the seven letters that our Lord Jesus sent to the seven churches in Revelation 2-3. Oh Lord, we humbly leave this matter at Your throne. We trust You and believe that because You are merciful, You will not bring divine judgment upon America until it is too late for repentance to take place in this land (2 Peter 3:8-9). Only You know when Your Spirit can no longer strive with Americans (Genesis 6:3). Oh God, have mercy on America!

Oh Lord, above everything else, we want You to be glorified. We are asking for mercy upon America and a revival in the land because we want to reach Americans with the gospel of Jesus Christ. We know that the day of Your divine judgment upon America and the entire world will come. May Your peace rest in our souls as You keep us in Your care as we wait for the moment when that judgment will come, or we rest in Your holy presence with You in Your heaven.

"And the Spirit and the bride [the church] say Come. And let him that heareth say, Come. And let him that is athirst come. And whosoever will, let him take the water of life freely." (Revelation 22:17) "Even so, come, Lord Jesus" (Revelation 22:20). Amen.

ENDNOTES

Chapter 2

1   John F. MacArthur, Jr.: *The Vanishing Conscience*, (Dallas: Word Publishing, 1994), 37.

Chapter 4

1   Ibid., 11.

Chapter 5

1   Ibid., 107.

Chapter 6

1   David Kupelian: *Whistleblower, The Left's War on Common Sense*, (Medford, OR: WND, July 2017), 7.

2   Ibid., 7.

Chapter 7

1   http://www. albert-mohler.com/2016/01/20/
     the-scandal-of-biblicalilliteracy-its-our-problem-4/.

Chapter 8

1   www.mediaed.org.

Chapter 9

1   Merrill F. Unger, <u>Demons in the World Today</u>, (Wheaton: Cloverdale House Publishers, 1971), 28, 30.

Chapter 10

1   www.thetruthwins.com.

2   John F. MacArthur, Jr.: *The Vanishing Conscience*, (Dallas: Word Publishing, 1994), 38.

Chapter 11

1   Merrill F. Unger, <u>Demons in the World Today</u>, (Wheaton: Cloverdale House Publishers, 1971), 30

2   Ibid., 28.

ABOUT THE AUTHOR

Mike Wingfield and his wife, Joyce, have been married for fifty years. They have two adult children and five grandchildren. Mike has been in the Christian ministry for more than forty-six years. He is a 1975 Master of Divinity honor graduate of Grace Theological Seminary in Winona Lake, Indiana. He was a pastor for twenty-five years in four churches in Indiana, Ohio, Virginia, and Tennessee. Since 1997, he has served as the founder and full-time director of Prophecy Today Ministries, P.O. Box 13006, Roanoke, Virginia, 24030-3006.

In the last thirty-four years he has traveled to the Middle East twenty-three times and has become familiar with the political, social, economic, and spiritual trends in the region. His careful study of the prophetic Scriptures, traveling experiences, and Scriptural analysis of world events, give him a keen insight into current events. Since 1997, his conference ministry has included more than 500 prophetic conferences in more than 200 churches in twenty-four states. His ministry has also included New Zealand, Canada, and Poland. His Bible prophecy newsletter has broad circulation throughout the U.S. and is available on the ministry website at www.ptnews.org. His messages are presented with PowerPoint, and demonstrate in a conservative way how current events are setting the stage for the final events of the end-times as recorded in the Bible.

In addition to his Bible prophecy conference and revival ministry, he also hosts annual tours to the lands of the Bible. These tours include Israel, Jordan, Egypt, Greece, and Turkey. He has also spoken in several schools, jails, nursing homes, plus several radio and TV talk shows. In recent years, his ministry has covered America from shore to shore – from Virginia to California and from Florida to Maine. He is the author of several books and the editor of the monthly 8-page *"PTNews"* newsletter (published since 1990).

In February 1993, a masked gunman, with a 12-gauge shotgun, forced entry into the Wingfield home. In the process of struggling with the masked intruder Mike was shot in both hands. In the following months, while Mike required numerous surgeries on both of his hands, the entire family had to go into hiding while detectives searched for the suspect. It took the police three and one-half years to solve the case. All evidence pointed to a young man, involved in drugs, who took his own life a few days after the shooting. This experience has had a profound impact upon Mike and his family, making them aware of the urgent need to share that God's grace is always sufficient in life's darkest hours.

OTHER PUBLICATIONS AND MINISTRY OPPORTUNITIES BY THE AUTHOR

Please send your request to: Prophecy Today Ministries, P.O. Box 13006, Roanoke, Virginia, 24030-3006. Or call: 1-540-798-7348 (Monday-Friday, 8 am – 4 pm EST)

PTNews- eight-page newsletter published ten times annually
Mike is the author and editor of this newsletter that focuses upon helping the believer develop a proper biblical worldview as it relates to the prophetic Scripture. Mike literally interprets Scripture and writes from his theological pre-tribulation and pre-millennial perspective. This newsletter enjoys broad circulation throughout the United States and is available on his ministry website: www.ptnew.org

Book (26 pages)- *Cremation – The Pagan's Choice* (published in 2018)
This publication examines biblical history and what believers have been saying and practicing for 4,000 years about the proper burial of the deceased. Cremation has been consistently rejected by the Old Testament Jewish people and the New Testament believers in the church. In his book, Mike examines why cremation is not God's choice for the final treatment of the human body.

Book: (57 pages)- *How to Know You Are Saved* (published in 2018)
In this publication Mike explores the biblical answer to this most important question – How can a person know for sure they are saved and will go to heaven? Using the biblical epistle of 1 John, he guides the reader through

nine vital questions that everyone needs to ask and then answer from the Bible.

Tours to the Holy Land

Mike also conducts annual tours to the lands of the Bible. For more information about one of his upcoming tours please go to www.ptnews.org or contact us for a brochure. He has visited the Holy Land twenty-three times in the last thirty-four years.

Speaking Availability

Mike would be glad to schedule your church for a speaking engagement. If you are interested please contact our office.